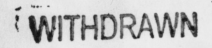

THE FOREIGN POLICIES OF
HERBERT HOOVER

THE FOREIGN POLICIES

OF HERBERT HOOVER

1929 – 1933

By

William Starr Myers

CHARLES SCRIBNER'S SONS · NEW YORK

CHARLES SCRIBNER'S SONS · LTD · LONDON

1940

857

april 1940

PREFACE

IN THE YEAR 1935 Mr. Walter H. Newton and I wrote a book entitled *The Hoover Administration—a Documented Narrative*. After conference with Mr. Hoover, we decided to omit therefrom all discussion of foreign affairs. This omission is supplied in the present book. Mr. Hoover has placed at my disposal unreservedly the use of his private papers contained in the Hoover Library on War, Revolution and Peace at Stanford University, also his own papers at his home in Palo Alto. This work is in large part based on these papers, and I have expressed my views with complete freedom. For this reason, these same views are my own, and neither he nor those others who have kindly assisted me by advice and information are in any way responsible for them.

I have attempted to give a survey of the Hoover policies as seen from the White House, that is to say, as he personally formulated them, and strove to carry through his far-reaching plans for the advancement of the interests of the United States, and for the furtherance of the cause of peace and human happiness throughout the world. This book, therefore, is in no sense a complete account of the foreign policies of the Hoover Administration. The restrictions on the use of govern-

v

mental material and other matters of present confidence
make such a definitive account impossible for some years
to come. But I feel that the time has come to make plain
just what the special Hoover policies were. They reflect
a philosophy enunciated by him more than twenty years
ago and reiterated since then with characteristic consistency.

This is not a biography of Mr. Hoover, but it should
be stated that no man has ever occupied the Presidency
with such a previous intimate acquaintance and experience with foreign peoples and their governments. Before the Great War, as a leading engineer and along
with his American practice, he had directed great works
in Russia, China, Japan, the British Empire, and other
European countries. Such enterprises were of necessity
in constant contact with the political, economic and
social forces of those countries. After 1914, he served
as head of the Belgian Relief which was in itself a kind
of independent power, and in constant touch with government officials in Germany, England and France.

When the United States entered the war Mr. Hoover
became a member of President Wilson's War Council
and as the head of the Allied Food Council he was again
brought into close contact with international problems.
For a year after the Armistice he was an executive head
and at times Chairman of the Supreme Economic Council representing all the Allied governments. That body
was engaged under his direction in the reconstruction

of the economic life, transportation, commerce, relief, credits, etc., of over twenty nations. Here, likewise, he was in daily touch with these governments. Never before has any single American been plunged so deeply into the life of European countries.

As Secretary of Commerce from 1922 to 1928, Mr. Hoover was again in continued contact and consultation in all our problems of foreign relations. He served on the Advisory Committee of the first Naval Reduction Conference, the War Debt Commissions, etc. Thus for over thirty years he had intimate understanding of foreign affairs.

I desire now to express my deep thanks to Doctor Nathan van Patten, Director of the Libraries of Stanford University, who showed me many and signal favors during my research among the papers in the Hoover Library on War, Revolution and Peace, and likewise to Miss Suda L. Bane, Archivist of the Herbert Hoover Archives for her invaluable assistance. The manuscript has been read in whole, or in part, by Honorable William R. Castle, of Washington, D. C., and by my colleagues, Professor Dana G. Munro and Professor Harold H. Sprout of Princeton University. Their suggestions and their criticism have been invaluable, and I am under deep obligations to them. The Rt. Hon. Malcolm MacDonald has graciously permitted the use of personal letters from his father, the late Ramsay MacDonald, to Mr. Hoover. My daughter and secre-

PREFACE

tary, Margaret Myers, has been faithful, painstaking and accurate, and her help in writing this book and preparing it for publication has been an essential part of the work. Finally, and as always, the encouragement and sympathetic interest of my wife has been constant and unfailing.

WILLIAM STARR MYERS.

Princeton, January 22, 1940.

CONTENTS

ix

CONTENTS

THE FOREIGN POLICIES OF
HERBERT HOOVER

I

PROBLEMS OF PEACE—1917-1929

HERBERT HOOVER is a realist. He was born in a family whose religion, that of the Society of Friends or Quakers, is characterized by deep spirituality combined with hard common sense. He was schooled in the experience of necessity and the difficulties of a youth lacking the abundance of material resources. But his inheritance was the best for a boy who was to become a self-made man of the most successful type. It gave him an endowment of physical strength, force of character, and mental ability which he was to use to the utmost, for he also brought to the use a deep sense of duty, an active conscience, an abiding sense of justice, and real human sympathy. In every sense he may be denoted a "typical Quaker."

Hoover's education at Stanford University and his experience as a mining engineer—a profession that carried him repeatedly to all parts of the world and caused him to deal with all sorts and kinds of people—but added to his realistic approach to facts. And he never lost his idealism, unselfishness, and human sympathy. All these things must be remembered when the career and the accomplishments of Herbert Hoover are under discussion and evaluation, for they form the background of all his later activities.

1

Both by theory and conviction, as well as religious training, Hoover has been a man of peace. But his idea of peace has been the result of a masterful handling of realities and not the weak emotionalism of the idealistic and inexperienced enthusiast. He was no pacifist. As he expressed it: "Preparedness for defense is the best insurance of peace." Precipitated by events into the midst of the war activities in 1914, and that without his own plan or volition, he saw at first hand the horrors of the gigantic world conflict, and the memories of these horrors have haunted him ever since. Although he at once arose to a position of great power and authority as the head of the humanitarian movement which so successfully fed and warmed the bodies of the Belgian and other war-ridden peoples, his unselfish devotion to American interests never faltered.

At a time of great crisis (July 20, 1917) he wrote to Joseph P. Tumulty, Secretary to President Wilson:[1] "If there ever was a time when decent men should hold up the President's hands it is right now. If I had any ambition other than that our Country under the great leadership of the President should carry this ... I should get more annoyed." But Hoover showed his real thought as well as the deep springs underlying his character by adding: "On the other hand this is the time when stock needs to be taken by every man in service to determine the moment when he becomes a liability to the

[1]Manuscript letter.

2

President and not an asset. The moment this occurs, and it must occur in war conditions to every man in important administrative post, then he should efface himself. My anxiety therefore is only to determine this moment." This statement is characteristic of Hoover, the man and the patriot, but not at this time a practical politician.

During the hectic days of the Paris Conference and the negotiation of the ill-starred and impossible Peace of Versailles, Hoover was a keen observer and never lost his sense of proportion. Although at the center of things, both at home and abroad, and well informed as to the course events were taking, he became alarmed and apprehensive with regard to the future. President Wilson, no matter what his abilities and how high his ideals, was enmeshed in the tangled net of European diplomacy. At times he was the perfect antithesis to Hoover for he allowed his idealism to becloud his sense of the realities. Inexperienced and unaccustomed to such wiles and double dealing as is the common change on the counter of European diplomacy, at times he was almost helpless in the hands of his professedly friendly and allied opponents.

Hoover during this time wrote several memoranda at the request of President Wilson which are of extreme importance. Thus, as early as the ill-fated Armistice Day, November 11, 1918, he said:[2] ". . . our en-

2The following quotations taken from manuscript.

3

tering into a joint Inter-Allied pool for the purpose of distributing all of the world's wheat until the middle of 1920, fills me with complete horror. Of all the import wheat in the world, seventy per cent must come from the Western Hemisphere and I assume that we would be called upon to finance it and to place the distribution of it in the hands of a body that we could not control. I can see no objective in such a plan as I believe there is sufficient wheat for the world to get through with, unless it is the intention to use this control of the prime necessity of life to dominate other measures in the world . . . on the subject of arrangements which the English may set up in London for provisioning the world with our foodstuffs and on our credit, I have similar reaction. Both of these . . . bring me to express to you the urgency of a definition of our principles in these matters, to be conveyed to the Allied governments in order that I and the other agents of the government in Europe may be able to act in entire unison with your own views."

Hoover now expressed in no uncertain terms what became an underlying principle of all his foreign policies from that time to the present day which is that in the Pauline sense we should be in the world but not of it. He always has maintained that we could preserve our national integrity and independence of action but yet co-operate in the meeting of great world problems and in the helping toward a sound and practical settlement of political and economic conditions. With usual farsightedness he saw the inevitable threat to our national welfare and added: "the Inter-Allied councils hitherto set up in Europe were entirely for the purpose of guiding Inter-Allied relations during the period of the war and any extension of their functions either by way of their control of our relations to other nations or the extension of their present functions beyond peace, cannot be entertained by us; all relationship involving the use of American food or credit for the people of other nations than the Allies themselves, must await . . . so far as any such supplies or interest of the United States is concerned. I believe that the settlement of this question requires some specific statement from you."

The Allied Governments, suffering under a form of shell-shock or nervous exhaustion due to the ghastly experiences of the four long war years, were giving way to their feelings of revenge and treating their defeated enemies in a manner which, although possible of defense upon principles of abstract justice, was only destined to cause dire trouble in the future, and to the neutrals as well. All of this offended both Hoover's common sense and sense of what was practical. He expressed this in another strong letter to President Wilson under date of Paris, February 4, 1919. Said he: "There is no right in the law of God or man that we should longer continue to starve neutrals now that we have a surplus of food." Never hesitating to come to the point, Hoover continued as follows in terms of specific indictment and clear warning. The events of the past twenty years have fully justified his statements. "The French, by obstruction of every financial measure that we can propose to the feeding of Germany in the attempt to compel us to loan money to Germany for this purpose, have defeated every step so far for getting them the food which we have been promising for three months . . . we are actually furnishing food to points in Austria at the expense of government that could be taken care of by private individuals if they could revive their foreign credit without enemy trade restrictions, blockade, and censorship, on commercial transactions."

Hoover then objected to a force which has been the bête noire of himself and many another high-minded statesman, who has wished to conduct the affairs of government on a basis of strict business efficiency. As a business executive of high standing he was especially sensitive to the ills of governmental and political bureaucracy. He complained that American objectives were "constantly defeated by one bureaucratic and special self-interest after another of various governments, and I can assure you that the blockade against neutrals and the Southwest is being used today for purely economic ends, when its sole justification was for the protection and furtherance of military opera-

6

tion which justification is now gone. . . .Any reference
to a given department in any government will in many
cases receive a negative opinion from individuals, simply because of interest in the self-perpetuation of bureaucracy or special interests of government or trade
in a desire to continue the use of this weapon for aims
entirely apart from the war. I am confident that no
action is possible except of a mandatory character
from the top."

As the months passed Hoover viewed with ever-grow-
ing apprehension the negotiations and events that culminated at Versailles. He could not resist another protest to President Wilson and on June 4, 1919, he
wrote a statement of his views to that harassed and
often-confused individual. Hoover pointed out that of
course he had no part in treaty making and for that
reason, and from the independent sources of information he had enjoyed, he had much opportunity for
objective observation. He urged that from an American
point of view we had been fighting autocracy and militarism and he felt that the paramount issues of the
day were to secure stability of government in Europe,
the establishment of democracy in Germany, and of *a*
league of nations which might be able further to cor-
rect international wrongs. Significantly he said: "I feel
that even if Germany signed the present terms, we
would not secure stability." After objecting to specific matters of injustice, Hoover added that he thought

7

these had been forced into the treaty against the wishes of the American negotiators, since there had been "a tendency to yield on these points because of the belief that the very survival of 200 million people revolved around early conclusion of these negotiations and the return of these populations to production, and that time and economic forces would remedy the worst phases." The accuracy of this judgment is vindicated by the process, twenty years later, which the world has been undergoing while "time and economic forces" are remedying the wrongs.

Herbert Hoover has been a wide and assiduous reader of history and has not failed to draw his lessons therefrom. Although at this time he was not versed in the wiles of practical politics as he has become during more recent years, yet he understood certain results of partisan politics as shown by many historical examples. He therefore wrote a very significant letter under date of Paris, March 11, 1919, to Colonel Edward M. House, at that time a member of the American Commission to Negotiate Peace. This letter likewise was as significant as those above quoted since it shows Hoover's rectitude, sincerity, and personal courage in meeting unfair and partisan attacks.

He called the attention of Colonel House to the fact that, due to the present political situation in the United States, Congress undoubtedly would proceed now to devote itself to an investigation of the conduct of the war.

This investigation would be: "a mixture of demagoguery, politics and sincerity of desire to maintain a high standard of administration." Owing to the nature of such investigations, it was often difficult to reach the truth since they are "so often colored with prejudice, political trickery, and self-advertising." In fact, they are "likely to besmirch the reputation of the American people to the whole world." After this accurate forecast of the general smearing process of which he himself was to be a prime victim in the coming years, Hoover continued to a further forecast of the proper method of meeting such untruthful propaganda. He stated that the war officials of the United States Government probably would handle some forty billion of dollars within the short period of two years. "They have mobilized an entire nation, not only for military action but for industrial and social concentration, and to my positive knowledge with a freedom from dishonesty and with an efficiency not equalled by another country engaged in this war." Although himself in politics a Republican of long standing, he set aside political partisanship and without hesitation paid this tribute to the Administration of Woodrow Wilson under Democratic party leadership.

Hoover's suggestion, in order to meet unfair and partisan criticism, was that Wilson as President should appoint a tribunal "composed of independent men of pre-eminent character who have themselves been free from administrative work during the war, who will sit as a commission to investigate the conduct of war." By this means the American people would be "freed from perpetually recurrent scandal and traduction at hands of demagogues by having some honorable acquittance and discharge of our case." This would tend to offset "that profound American ambition to advertise our weaknesses to the world without any appreciation of our strength." While this suggestion unfortunately was not accepted in its entirety, it shows characteristic judgment and planning on the part of the writer of the letter.

It is merely a restatement of well-known fact to say that when actual warfare ceased in Europe that Continent was facing political, economic and social chaos. President Wilson authorized Hoover to institute what might be called a second intervention in order to organize Europe and to carry over its people until the harvest and the final establishment of peace. For this purpose the Supreme Economic Council was organized with members from the cabinets of all the Allied Governments. Hoover was an American member, was the effective administrative head, and was in rotation the Chairman. This Council controlled all Allied shipping, and through the blockade practically directed the credit and food supplies of the world. Its purpose also was to restore economic life, to prevent famine, pestilence and anarchy, and to stop the spread of bolshevism.

Thus an added purpose was to enable peace to be made successfully. This gave him a rare opportunity to come into close contact with people of all sorts and kinds, from the highest to the lowest, and to gain a keen appreciation of their desperate problems. Hoover himself stated on many subsequent occasions that the experiences during this time of service resulted in two dominant convictions.[3] The first of these resulted from "contact with stupendous social ferment and revolution in which Europe was attempting to find a solution for all its social ills by practical experiments in Marxian Socialism." Said Hoover, in crisp and cutting words, "this whole philosophy is bankrupting itself from a startling quarter in the extraordinary lowering of productivity of industrial commodities to a point that, until the recent realization of this bankruptcy, was below the necessity for continued existence of their millions of people."

The second of his above mentioned convictions was the result of earlier life and training but "greatly hardened" into a further "appreciation of the enormous distance that we of America have grown away from Europe in the century and a half of our national existence, in our outlook on life, our relations toward our neighbors and our social and political ideals." He added that this Americanism was of such supreme importance that it did not permit us to offer ourselves for ex-

[3]Address at dinner of the Institute of Mining and Metallurgical Engineers, September 16, 1919.

11

periments in social diseases or to abandon the moral leadership we had undertaken of restoring order in the world.

This latter statement was caused by Hoover's observation, noted months before,[4] that there was a tendency on the part of the American people "to return to their instinctive desire for separation from European entanglements beyond co-operation with their associates in winding up the war." Furthermore they "must be impressed constantly with their national duty in participation in the helping of the Allies and other countries of Europe from the effects of the war." Hoover stated his view that there was "no way through which the national conscience can be so awakened and retained constantly upon this problem as through their participation in a matter which so strikes national imagination . . . that by self-denial on their part . . . they should be providing food stuffs for millions of people in Europe." In accordance with his life-long belief in the essential soundness of character of the American people, he emphatically stated that "any action on their part must be voluntary and not compulsory."

It goes without saying that one of the most vital and pressing problems facing Hoover and those associated with him in the relief of famine and other eco-

---

[4]Statement furnished by Messrs. Hoover and Davis to the Committee appointed by the Allied Premiers to consider relief matters, Dec. 10, 1918.

nomic distress was caused by Russia and the Bolshevist terrorists who were in control of that unhappy country. His summing up of the situation, his judgment of the real character and value of this radical, Socialistic and Communistic movement are of special significance in the light of developments since that time. As early as the spring of 1919 he agreed to the proposal that Russia should be fed, subject to the guarantees that this should be done through a strong neutral commission with complete justice of distribution and that the Bolsheviki should keep themselves within a definite circumscribed area and without military activities.

It is expedient to quote the exact words of Herbert Hoover in his early evaluation of the Soviet Government and its policies. Said he in a statement under the date of April 18, 1919:[5] "The economic and political situation inside Bolsevik Russia today is about as bad as it can be. Through the agents of the Food organization, we have made a great deal of inquiry into this internal situation. Several primary facts stand out with great vividness. The first is that Russia is not only normally an extremely well fed country but formerly exported as much food as did the United States, yet today her people are dying in thousands from starvation for no other reason in the world than the fool idea that the processes of production and distribution can be broken down in a country and the popuation still

[5]Manuscript copy.

live. The second outstanding fact is that this mixture of theorists, dreamers and murderers that comprise the Bolshevik Government have themselves at last to some degree realized the infinite calamity that they have brought on their people and are themselves floundering around endeavoring to restore the normal processes of production and distribution."

Also, and of equal importance with the above, is Hoover's estimate of the real, "old-fashioned" economic Liberalism as a basis of American institutions which he gave in summary in a letter to President Wilson on March 28, 1919. It is especially significant in the light of the subsequent sound and constructive policies inaugurated by Herbert Hoover when, as President of the United States, he was faced with the national problem caused by the depression which began in the autumn of 1929.[6] "We must all agree that our processes of production and distribution, the outgrowth of a hundred generations, in the stimulation to individual initiative, the large equality of opportunity and infinite knowledge of mind and body, while not perfect, come about as near perfection as is possible from the mixture of avarice, ambition, altruism, intelligence, ignorance and education, of which the human animal is today composed. The Bolshevik's land of illusion is that he can perfect these human qualities by destroying the basic processes of production and distribution

[6]Manuscript copy of letter.

instead of devoting himself to securing a better application of the collective surplus."

It was at this time and in this same letter that Hoover stated that: "We cannot even remotely recognize this murderous Bolshevist tyranny without stimulating actionist radicalism in every country in Europe and without transgressing on every National idea of our own." And it was the same conviction that caused the nonrecognition policy with regard to Russia that was maintained with consistency by Presidents Wilson, Harding, Coolidge and Hoover and by their Secretaries of State—Colby, Hughes, Kellogg, and Stimson.

Herbert Hoover during this period early became aware of Woodrow Wilson's plan for the League of Nations and that this League was to be completely bound up with the Peace Treaty, then in process of negotiation. In accordance with prevailing American convictions and traditions, Hoover did not believe that the United States should become involved in European politics, as already stated. He became very apprehensive as he saw the development of Woodrow Wilson's personal policies as they dominated the actions of the American Peace Commission in Paris. These apprehensions caused Hoover to write a lengthy memorandum to President Wilson on April 11, 1919,[7] nearly two months before peace was signed at Versailles. After

[7]Manuscript letter later published in pamphlet form with collection of documents, entitled *Some Notes on the League of Nations*, by Herbert Hoover.

15

discussing some immediate questions of American participation in European economic commissions, Hoover continued:

"I am convinced that there has grown up since the Armistice the policy, perhaps unconscious, but nevertheless effective, of dragging the United States into every political and economic question in Europe and constantly endeavoring to secure pledges of economic and political support from us in return for our agreeing to matters which we consider for their common good, where we have no interest. They are constantly using us as a stalking horse economically and politically, solely in the interests of internal political groups within the Allied Governments. These objectives and interests may be perfectly justified from their point of view. But it forces us into violations of our every instinct and into situations that our own people will never stand. For instance, I don't see how we can remain in these enforcement commissions unless we participate in the military enforcement with its enormous cost and risk. And the tendency will aways be to exact the political objectives with the military strength of the United States as a background.

"I have the feeling that revolution in Europe is by no means over. The social wrongs in these countries are far from solution and the tempest must blow itself out, probably in enormous violence. Our people are not prepared for us to undertake the military policing of

16

Europe while it boils out its social wrongs. I have no doubt that if we could undertake to police the world and had the wisdom of statesmanship to see its gradual social evolution, we could be making a great contribution to civilization. But I am certain that the American people are not prepared for such a measure and I am also sure that if we remain in Europe with military force, tied in an alliance which we have never undertaken, we should be forced into a storm of repression of revolution, and we would be forced in under terms of co-ordination with other people that would make our own independence of action wholly impossible.

"It grows upon me daily that the United States is the one great moral reserve in the world today. We cannot maintain the independence of action through which this reserve is to be maintained if we allow ourselves to be dragged into European entanglements over a period of years. In my view, if the Allies cannot be brought to adopt peace on the basis of the 14 points, we should retire from Europe, lock, stock and barrel. We should lend to the whole world our economic and moral strength or the world will swim in a sea of misery and disaster worse than the Dark Ages. If they cannot be brought to accept peace on this basis, our national honor is at stake and we should have to make peace independently and retire. I know of nothing in letter or spirit of any statement of your own, or in the

14 points, that directly or indirectly ties the United States to carry on this war through the phase of enforcement or the multitudinous demands and intrigues of a great number of other governments and their officials.

"It does appear to me that your conception of the League of Nations is with view to a great moral Court, where these difficulties could be threshed out, but if we sit as one of the prosecutors, the Court will have no judge."

To this Wilson replied four days later on April 15, 1919, that he was "very much impressed" by Hoover's objections and that he agreed with him but feared that the United States could not "escape membership" on the Financial Commission of Reparations, since the latter undoubtedly would need an umpire. That Wilson did not follow Hoover's advice, taken in its entirety, may be considered to be one of the many causes of the tragic defeat of President Wilson during the next year.

Following the signature of the Treaty of Peace, Hoover was faced with a real dilemma. While he believed in some form of international organization for purposes of conference and co-operation, he did not believe in the League of Nations *as organized*. But he saw the imperative need for peace and the need for getting it quickly. For these reasons he came out in favor of the League and urged its acceptance by the Senate with the minor changes, through reservations, offered in that body. Due to President Wilson's stub-

bornness and lack of conciliation, probably intensified
by his ill-health and nervous exhaustion, the matter
came to a "dead end" so far as the Democratic party
was concerned[8] and Hoover, being a Republican, naturally felt that the best opportunity for constructive
action lay in a victory for the Republican party.

It was during the presidential campaign of 1920
that Hoover made a public statement of his views on
the League of Nations controversy which was published
in the *Chicago Daily News* for September 15th. First
of all, he stressed the fact that he had "not forgotten
the 50,000,000 human beings who have died because of
this war, or the death toll which will stream from it for
many years to come." In order at least to try to lessen
the dangers of future wars "we require cooperative
international action—'a' League." Also, Hoover considered the essential principle of such a League to be
"a continuous council of men representing the authority and confidence of their own countries in continuous
service to mitigate the causes which give rise to war."
This body should need "no more powers than public
opinion." Furthermore such a body could perform great
service to the entire world in the building up of international action, concerned with "the protection of life
and private property at sea, the spread of contagious

[8]Hoover wrote President Wilson on November 19, 1919, urging him
to accept the reservations to the League of Nations' Covenant as
passed by the Senate, adding—"I am impressed with the desperate
necessity of early ratification." (Copy of manuscript letter.)

19

disease, the development of international communications." It will be seen that the question of private property at sea easily developed into Hoover's idea, which he repeatedly has stressed since that time, that food ships should enjoy immunity from blockade and capture in time of war.

Hoover now met the issues of the current presidential campaign in the following specific words. "I see no reason why such a body should have any power that leads to supergovernment, or that in any way minimizes the very essential principle of nationalism upon which our patriotism and progress is founded. I do not believe that interest in the welfare of our neighborhood undermines our family life." His reason for supporting the Republican ticket was stated as follows: "I have no faith in a party (Democratic) that will delay the world's peace for over a year by obstinately refusing to meet the public demand over points of method that even they now appear to question by promising some kind of reservations. I have confidence in the assurances of the Republican party to bring about an agreement to install the major purposes of a League, and that under President Harding we will have an era of practical statesmanship that will quickly dispose of the problem in a large broadminded way, by building upon the present structure—and then get to our great job —economic reconstruction."

The elections of the following November resulted in

the overwhelming success of the Republican ticket and
Warren G. Harding became President of the United
States on March 4, 1921, while Calvin Coolidge became Vice-President. President Harding offered Hoover the portfolio of the Department of Commerce and
thus the latter became a member of the Cabinet and
began his career in active American politics, with the
added task of conforming his ideas of administration
to the "practical" needs of the latter. But he did not
forget his interest in the maintenance of peace and he
made many addresses on the subject. It was during
the period of this service that the general treaty for
the renunciation of war was under negotiation in which
the Secretary of State of the United States and the
Minister of Foreign Affairs of France took a leading
part. As a result, President Coolidge in April, 1928,
directed Secretary Frank B. Kellogg to propose to the
nations of the world that they should enter into a
binding agreement in which they should "condemn re-
course to war for the solution of international controversies and renounce it as an instrument of national
policy in their relations with one another." Furthermore the settlement, or solution, of all disputes or conflicts "shall never be sought except by pacific means."

It was only after the lapse of more than a year that
the Kellogg-Briand Peace Pact could go into effect.
This carried it over into the Administration of Herbert
Hoover, now become President of the United States.

On July 24, 1929, he issued a Proclamation declaring the Pact in effect and made an address at the White House on the occasion of the proclamation.[9] In this address he stated that the Pact was "a proposal to the conscience and idealism of civilized nations. It suggested a new step in international law, rich with meaning, pregnant with new ideas in the conduct of world relations. It represented a platform from which there is instant appeal to the public opinion of the world as to specific acts and deeds. . . . I congratulate this assembly, the states it represents, and indeed, the entire world upon the coming into force of this additional instrument of humane endeavor to do away with war as an instrument of national policy and to obtain by pacific means alone the settlement of international disputes." Both ex-President Coolidge and ex-Secretary of State Frank B. Kellogg were present on this occasion, since it was during their administration of the foreign affairs of the United States that the Peace Pact was initiated.

Subsequent events give a note of irony to the following radiogram which had been received by President Hoover the preceding day from Paul von Hindenburg, President of the German Reich: "On the occasion of the going into effect of the Pact for the Renunciation of War in the creation of which the United States of America had so prominent a part, I express to you,

[9]See text of this address in "State Papers of Herbert Hoover," ed. by W. S. Myers (1934), Vol. I, pp. 78–80. Future references to this work will be under the title of "State Papers."

Mr. President, the most heartfelt congratulations. I cherish the hope that the Pact will prove its strength in the shaping of the relations between the nations and contribute to securing the peace of the world on the foundation of right."[10]

To make the Pact effective, negotiation of further treaties providing methods for the peaceful settlement of disputes was required. During the Hoover Administration twenty-five new treaties of arbitration and seventeen new treaties of conciliation were entered into. Also, "several score other treaties" all of which contributed to the development of peaceful relations with other countries[11] were negotiated, covering slavery, narcotics, commerce, aviation, and merchant marine. Another matter inherited by President Hoover was the problem of ratification by the United States Senate of the Protocol establishing the Court of International Justice, otherwise known as the "World Court." Since this was a subject of several years' controversy, which

[10]MS. Copy. President Hoover always kept in close touch with his associates in administration, whether business or governmental. Illustration of this is found in the following MS. letter from Secretary of State Henry L. Stimson, which reads as follows—"July 23, 1929. My dear Mr. President: I am herewith returning your revised draft of your address to be given tomorrow on the occasion of the Proclamation of the Treaty for the Renunciation of War. I have read it over and I must say I do not see how it could be improved. I have also had it checked as far as concerns the names of the countries which have signed the Treaty, those which have adhered to the Treaty and deposited their ratifications and those who have carried out all the necessary requirements for adherence with the exception of the deposit of their instrument of ratification with this Government. I am, my dear Mr. President, Faithfully yours, (signed) H. L. Stimson."

[11]Ray Lyman Wilbur and Arthur Mastic Hyde, *The Hoover Policies*, 1937, p. 587. Further references to this work will be made under the title "Wilbur and Hyde."

even yet is not settled, it will be considered in the next chapter.

NOTE

Policies towards Russia during the Hoover Administration were simple and direct. Despite pressure from the totalitarian "Liberals" and the propaganda of the Communist government, Hoover refused to recognize the government of Russia. This propaganda was also backed by certain business interests who constantly emphasized the supposed trade advantages to the United States from recognition.

Hoover was familiar with Russia on account of his professional contacts prior to the war. His abhorrence of the terrorism of the Czarist government had been deepened by this experience to an extent far greater than that of the ordinary American. He rejoiced when the Czarist government was overthrown and a liberal democratic régime was established. He felt that the Russian people were to have some opportunity for real development. With the fall of this democratic régime under Kerensky, and its replacement by the Communists, Hoover was under no illusions but knew that it meant the extinction of hope for the Russian people so long as their power lasted. He was not carried away by the rejoicing of the totalitarian "Liberals" of the world who claimed that this was the opening of a new and better day for Russia.

Wilson, like Hoover, was firm in the belief that there was no true liberalism in the Soviet régime. The execution of thousands of democratic leaders in Russia, the general butchery, and the extinction of all liberties should have been enough to warn true Liberals of the dangers.

During the peace negotiations in Paris, Hoover was called upon by Wilson for advice on American relations to Russia. He formulated this advice in the several memoranda heretofore quoted, which was based on his wide knowledge of the Russian people and of the character and meaning of Communism. After his return to the United States in 1920 he wrote in a book, entitled "American Individualism," an appeal to intellectual Liberals to uphold the fundamentals of American life as opposed to Communism and totalitarianism.

But the so-called "Liberals" in the United States made "recognition of Russia" a slogan of "Liberalism." One of the most curious events in the whole history of Liberalism was this support of the recognition of Russia and also the constant defense of the Soviet régime. These "Liberals" formed one of the bitterest groups among the critics of Hoover, and used against him all of the well-known expedients of the Communistic type of propaganda.

In Hoover's view they were totally ignorant of the real fundamental purposes both of Communism and of true Liberalism. His belief was that a régime and

25

government with such a record of terror, tyranny, and murder should not receive the dignity of recognition among nations, and certainly not from a democracy. Recognition would rivet the hold of less than 2,000,000 Communists upon the 150,000,000 people in Russia, would give to Communism respectability in the world, and would open the floodgates to propaganda and Communist organization in the United States.

That Hoover was right was shown soon after the recognition of the Communist government of Russia by the Roosevelt Administration. Communist activities at once flooded the United States in open coalition with so-called "Liberal" groups. A host of "fellow-traveller" organizations and the penetration and disruption of many American labor unions are the result of this destructive coalition. The growth of this influence in the United States was later on exposed by Congressional investigation.

The true character was shown at last in the combination of Russia with Germany in the attempt to crush out free institutions by military force. The destruction of Czechoslovakia and Poland and the attack upon Finland are but parts of the story. The American people should be grateful to Hoover that, during his four years of administration, this country was protected from the penetration of Communist activities which have since brought about so much conflict and destruction in both the moral and the material welfare of the United States.

II

THE WORLD COURT

HERBERT HOOVER always has been strong in his support of the principle of the settlement of international disputes by means of judicial process. During the ten years preceding his election to the office of President of the United States, he had been a keen observer of the movement leading to the establishment of the World Court and also to the controversies that arose over the question of the United States becoming a member. He at all times strongly supported American adherence to it. Certain events connected with the activities of Elihu Root brought the issue immediately to his attention at the time of his inauguration on March 4, 1929. These events must be given in outline in order that the action taken by Hoover may be understood.[1]

A committee of ten jurists of international standing, of whom Elihu Root was one, met at The Hague in Holland in the year 1920 and drew up the "Statute of the Permanent Court of International Justice," otherwise known as the World Court Protocol. This treaty was submitted to the Senate by President Harding in February, 1923, but aroused bitter opposition among

[1] A clear and concise account of the relations of Mr. Root to these events, and the great services he rendered to the cause of international peace during this whole period, may be found in the *Life of Elihu Root* by Philip C. Jessup (1938), Vol. II, pp. 418–444.

those Senators who were opposed to the League of Nations and insisted that our adhesion to the Protocol would be merely "entering the League by a back door." They persisted in calling the tribunal the "League Court" and refused to bring the matter to a vote. Finally, after President Coolidge had recommended ratification in his annual message of December 2, 1925, the matter was taken up for debate. On January 27, 1926, the Senate ratified the Protocol, subject to five reservations, and also made a statement of two understandings. The most important part of these additions was the fifth reservation which restricted the right of the World Court to render advisory opinions except under strict provisions for publicity and due notice. Also the Court might not decide upon a request for an advisory opinion upon "any dispute or question in which the United States has or claims an interest" without the consent of this country.

A special meeting of delegates from the states signatory to the World Court was called and met in Geneva the following September, 1926. At this time it was found that there was no difficulty about their accepting the Senate reservations with the exception of the fifth. It was here that the point of difference arose since foreign nations desired a clarification of the meaning of that portion of the reservation in which the United States mentioned possible claims of interest. American opponents of membership in the Court

were suspicious of the restrictive meaning of the same
words and fearful that any modification might add to
the danger of involvement of the United States in
world affairs. The Committee made suggestions with
regard to a possible solution of the problem but Court
opponents in the United States prevented any further
action in the matter. However, on December 14, 1928,
the Council of the League decided to invite a committee of experts to meet in Geneva for the purpose of
considering any necessary amendments to the Statute
which established the Court.[2] Elihu Root was invited
to become a member of the Committee. Although 84
years of age, Root felt impelled by a supreme sense
of duty to accept and did so. This caused at once the
question to arise whether or not the problem of the
American fifth reservation might be solved.

This happened during the closing days of the Coolidge Administration and Root first went to Washington for consultation with Frank B. Kellogg, Secretary
of State, and with a number of prominent Senators,
including the Republican Senator William E. Borah,
and the Democrats Claude A. Swanson, of Virginia,
and Thomas J. Walsh, of Montana. He already had
sketched out his ideas of a possible solution and this
received favorable consideration by the above mentioned individuals. "President-elect Hoover sent him
a cordial and confident message of farewell."[3]

[2]Jessup, *Elihu Root,* Vol. II, pp. 434–435.
[3]Jessup, *ibid.,* Vol. II, p. 435.

Root sailed for Europe on February 15 and arrived in Geneva about the 1st of March. He at once went actively to work in spite of the physical handicaps of poor health and advanced age and on March 4, the day of Hoover's inauguration, he cabled a full report to Secretary Kellogg who was continuing in office as Secretary of State until the arrival, from the Far East, of Henry L. Stimson who had accepted appointment to this position in the Cabinet of President Hoover. Root urged that: "It may be necessary to act very rapidly as the representatives of the signatories are now here for a meeting of the Council and at the end of this week they will leave. Before leaving here it is highly important that they reach favorable conclusions," regardless of the manner in which effect was to be given to those conclusions. Minor matters could be provided for when the protocol was redrafted after the removal of the main difficulty.

Root cabled the next day requesting authority, if the President should approve the draft of his proposal, and which is given below, to present it officially to the Secretary-General of the League of Nations. However, he wired again on March 7 stating that there was no need to trouble about authority since he had arranged for referring the matter to a committee of experts.

The suggested draft for a proposed working agreement was as follows:

"The Court shall not, without the consent of the

United States, render an advisory opinion touching any dispute to which the United States is not a party but in which it claims an interest or touching any question other than a dispute in which the United States claims an interest.

"The manner in which it shall be made known whether the United States claims an interest and gives or withholds its consent shall be as follows:

"Whenever, in the contemplation of request for an advisory opinion it seems to them desirable, the Council or assembly may invite an exchange of views with the United States and such exchange of views shall proceed with all convenient speed.

"Whenever a request for an advisory opinion comes to the Court the registrar shall notify the United States thereof among other states mentioned in the now existing article 73 of the Rules of Court stating a reasonable time limit fixed by the President within which a written statement by the United States concerning the request will be received.

"In case the United States shall, within the time fixed, advise the Court in writing that the request touches a dispute or question in which the United States has an interest and that the United States has not consented to the submission of the question; thereupon, all proceedings upon the question shall be stayed to admit of exchange of views between the United States and the proponents of the request and such exchange of views shall proceed with all convenient speed. If after such an exchange of views, either while a question is in contemplation or after a question has gone to the Court, it shall appear:

"(one) That no agreement can be reached as to whether the question does touch an interest of the United States within the true meaning of the second paragraph of this article; and,

"(two) That the submission of the question is still insisted upon after attributing to the objection of the United States the same force and effect as attaches to a vote against asking for the opinion given by a member of the League of Nations either in the Assembly or in the Council and if it also appears that the United States has not been able to find the submission of the question so important for the general good as to call upon the United States to forgo its objection in that particular instance, leaving the request to be acted upon by the Court without in any way binding the United States; then, it shall be deemed that owing to a material difference of view regarding the proper scope of the practice of requesting advisory opinions the arrangement now agreed upon is not yielding satisfactory results and that the exercise of the powers of withdrawal provided in article seven, hereof, will follow naturally without any imputation of unfriendliness or of unwillingness to cooperate generally for peace and good will."

Root included in his statement an exposition of the legal and theoretical principles involved in his proposed solution which dealt with technicalities of interpretation that might arise. The reply came that President Hoover considered the plan to be feasible and thought well of it. On the other hand, it was suggested that care must be taken not to arouse the susceptibilities of the Senate. For this purpose negotiations should be conducted with individual governments and not through the agency of the League at Geneva. As later stated by Philip C. Jessup, "it was ultimately decided that the Council would refer the whole matter to the Committee of Jurists and Root therefore never received any official representative authority. From first to last on this trip he was merely a private citizen, serving as an individual expert on an international committee."[4] During this whole period Hoover was well aware of the difficulties in the way of securing the acceptance by the Senate of any action interpretive of the fifth reservation which might be secured by Root at Geneva. He was very careful to stress the need for securing such changes in the Protocol of the World Court as would meet the objections which had been, or might be, raised in the Senate. He wrote a letter to Secretary Kellogg on March 8 following a conference with Senator Borah on the preceding evening. He states as follows:[5]

[4] *Ibid.*, Vol. II, p. 438.
[5] This and following letters from manuscripts.

33

"I have now had an opportunity of discussing Mr. Root's proposal with Senator Borah. My understanding is that Senator Borah is opposed to the Court undertaking any advisory opinions, and voted against our adherence to the Court for this reason. He also feels that Mr. Root's plan satisfies the requirements of the fifth reservation. He seems to feel that those who believe we should adhere to the Court subject to the reservations ought to be satisfied with Mr. Root's plan.

"Senator Borah still believes that the suggestion he made to Mr. Root that the statute should provide that no advisory opinions would be given in respect to non-members of the League would be a more effective method of action than the special program provided by Mr. Root."

Senator Walsh agreed in principle saying: "I approve of the draft sent by Senator Root intended as a modification of Reservation V, and am prepared to urge acceptance of it by the Senate in lieu of its draft, but the essentials could, in my judgment, be expressed in fewer words. With great deference I offer the following." As already stated these suggestions were largely on the basis of abridgment rather than change in the text of Root's suggestion.

Root's proposals, with certain minor revisions, were adopted by the Committee of Experts. After leaving Geneva, Root tarried a short time in Paris and London.

Hoover was aware that he must move slowly as President. It was evident that the proposal could not be passed in the Senate, until there was a change of views there. Hoover wanted to hold it for more favorable opportunity. Stimson, who was now Secretary of State, wished it pressed irrespective of this situation and represented that delay would be bad faith. On October 18, 1929, he wrote Stimson as follows:

"Dear Mr. Secretary:

"If you feel that the good faith of the United States is involved, I think you had better sign the protocol. I am afraid you will not be able to justify withholding it from Congress the next session if you do so, and I am in turn afraid that this would seriously impair our hope of securing adhesion to a naval treaty. I am, however, of course, prepared to go through with it if our promises are in any way in question.

"Yours faithfully,
(signed) "Herbert Hoover"

Hoover was proved to be right. It did not succeed in the Senate.

The following letter shows the extreme care and analytical thought that Hoover gave to the consideration of such problems. Under date of November 27 he wrote Secretary Stimson in part as follows, in order that their cordial agreement and understanding

35

upon the subject might have no unforeseen or unintentional interruption.

"Dear Mr. Secretary:

"Do we not negotiate with the League of Nations upon the subject of Advisory Opinions? If we claim an 'interest' and object for that reason, our objection is made to the League and not to the Court. If, notwithstanding our objection, the League asks for an advisory opinion, the Court must render it unless it finds that we have an actual interest in the controversy, as distinguished from a claim of interest. All that happens in case our claim is not allowed by the League is that we withdraw from the Court.

"The Amendment to the Statute of the Court applies, as I understand it, only to such cases as the Eastern Carelian case, and would not cover a case where we claim an interest only because the decision might create a precedent that at some future time might affect us.   "Yours faithfully,

(signed) "Herbert Hoover"

Evidently Hoover soon was thoroughly satisfied and therefore wrote Secretary Stimson that he authorized the latter to make the necessary arrangements for the signature on behalf of the United States on December 9, 1929, of the World Court Protocol. Hoover delayed the submission of the Protocol to the Senate in order to secure a better reception. The nomination of Ruth Hanna McCormick in the Republican primaries in Illinois of April, 1930, as a candidate for the United States Senate aroused vociferous claims by its opponents that it was caused by opposition to the World Court. While this was hotly denied by the champions of the latter, yet it was a possible danger signal and a sign to go slow. It was not until the latter part of the next year that Hoover felt it safe to undertake the task of securing ratification of the Protocol as modified by the changes secured through the efforts of Root. A careful tabulation of the daily papers submitted to Hoover, on December 8, 1930, showed the following: daily papers favorable to the World Court, 1357, with a circulation of 26,993,906; those opposed, 265, circulation 10,557,317; papers taking no stand, 58, with a circulation of 549,177. Encouraged by this evidence that his action would be in accordance with the public opinion of a large section of the people, Hoover submitted the Protocols to the Senate December 10, 1930, in which he stated[6] that:

"The provisions of the protocols free us frcm any entanglement in the diplomacy of other nations. We cannot be summoned before this Court, we can from time to time seek its services by agreement with other nations. These protocols permit our withdrawal from the Court at any time without reproach or ill-will.

[6]*State Papers*, Vol. I, p. 460, *et seq.*

"The movement for the establishment of such a court originated with our country. It has been supported by Presidents Wilson, Harding, and Coolidge; by Secretaries of State Hughes, Kellogg, and Stimson; it springs from the earnest seeking of our people for justice in international relations and to strengthen the foundations of peace.

"Through the Kellogg-Briand Pact we have pledged ourselves to the use of pacific means in settlement of all controversies. Our great nation, so devoted to peace and justice, should lend its co-operation in this effort of the nations to establish a great agency for such pacific settlements."

During all this time, through their usual lack of perspective or sense of appropriateness, also with a thorough misunderstanding, Hoover was hounded by the emotional and professional peace advocates who were attempting to force his hand, although he knew better than they what might be accomplished under the circumstances. The following telegram from a well-known pacifist is a good illustration of the irritating pin-pricks to which he was continually subjected.

"Syracuse, N. Y., Jan. 9, 1931

"The President:

"Persistent rumors you will try to stop incipient world court campaign by ruling out special Senate session. This would necessitate our turning campaign

38

from Senate to you to secure change your policy. Earnestly advise leaving Senate responsible. Our campaign is hardly begun compared with January and February.

(signed) "Frederick J. Libby."

In his message of December 10, 1931, Hoover again pressed the subject upon the attention of Congress:[7]

"In the past session of the Congress I transmitted to the Senate protocols providing for adherence by the United States to the Permanent Court of International Justice. Upon that occasion I expressed my views fully not only of the wisdom of such action, but that the safeguards against European entanglements stipulated for by the Senate had been in effect secured and the interest of the United States protected. I need not repeat that for over twelve years every President and every Secretary of State has urged this action as a material contribution to the pacific settlement of controversies among nations and the further assurance against war."

The opposition in the Senate was strong enough to prevent the matter coming to a vote. Meanwhile the time and attention of Hoover were so engrossed in his efforts to meet the ghastly results of the depression which began in the autumn of 1929, that he was compelled, perforce, to drop the matter. The question did not come up again until January, 1935, when his suc-

[7]State Papers, Vol. II, pp. 80-81.

cessor, Franklin D. Roosevelt, was defeated by opposition, led by William Randolph Hearst and his newspapers and aided by the Roman Catholic priest, Father Coughlin. The Senate refused ratification by the necessary two-thirds majority.

III

LATIN-AMERICAN RELATIONS

DURING the period between the November election and his inauguration in March, 1929, Hoover made a tour of the principal South American countries as President-elect, in order that he personally might exchange views with their officials and promote good-will among their people. This visit was introductory to a transformation in the hitherto strained Latin-American relations, which was accomplished under Hoover's leadership during the following four years. During his eight years as Secretary of Commerce Hoover had transformed the American trade service to those countries. He had not only introduced high skill into it, but also had built it up on a basis of mutual service to both sides. Also, he himself was familiar with our various South American trade problems.

He referred to this visit in his Inaugural address on March 4 at the Capitol by saying:[1] "I have lately returned from a journey among our sister Republics of the Western Hemisphere. I have received unbounded hospitality and courtesy as their expression of friendliness to our country. We are held by particular bonds of sympathy and common interest with them. They are each of them building a racial character and a culture

[1]*State Papers*, Vol. I, pp. 9–10.

41

which is an impressive contribution to human progress. We wish only for the maintenance of their independence, the growth of their stability, and their prosperity. While we have had wars in the Western Hemisphere, yet on the whole the record is in encouraging contrast with that of other parts of the world. Fortunately the New World is largely free from the inheritances of fear and distrust which have so troubled the Old World. We should keep it so."

A few weeks later Hoover took advantage of the occasion when he addressed the Gridiron Club of Washington, D. C., at its dinner on April 13, 1929, to repeat a declaration that he had repeatedly made on his trip to South America. This was especially opportune since the ambassadors and ministers from these countries were likewise guests on this occasion, Said he:[2] "These countries have recently extended to me and to many members of the American press the hospitality of their countries. Theirs was a hospitality which breathed good will and a desire to demonstrate that fundamental friendship to our country, which runs deep in the sense of all the people of the Western Hemisphere.

"And I wish to take this occasion to express the deep appreciation which is due the American correspondents who accompanied me upon that visit for the effectiveness and devotion with which they each of

[2]*State Papers*, Vol. I, pp. 29–30.

them interpreted our countrymen to our neighbors. They carried in person the inner thought of our countrymen that it is not size, wealth, or potency of the Nation—that it is progress of and service of a nation in the upbuilding of the institutions of freedom, its contribution to the growth of liberty, the development of humane relations, the advancement of the individual man—which measures the soul and might of nations.

"And in this connection of the relations of great and little nations may I mention one sinister notion, fear of which I detect in some sections of the press, as to policies of the United States bearing basically upon our relationships with our Latin-American neighbors? That is, fear of an era of the mistakenly called dollar diplomacy. The implications that have been colored by that expression are not a part of my conception of international relations. I can say at once that it never has been and ought not to be the policy of the United States to intervene by force to secure or maintain contracts between our citizens and foreign States or their citizens. Confidence in that attitude is the only basis upon which the economic cooperation of our citizens can be welcomed abroad. It is the only basis that prevents cupidity encroaching upon the weakness of nations—but, far more than this, it is the true expression of the moral rectitude of the United States."

This courageous declaration by President Hoover of the principles upon which he was to conduct our

Latin-American governmental policies was accompanied during the time of his administration by the abandonment of the Wilson policies of military intervention.

Certain specific results came from Hoover's goodwill visit. First of all he realized the vast importance of our relations with Latin America and determined, as far as possible, to appoint to those countries men of training in diplomatic work in order that relations might be carried on more smoothly and effectively than had been true in the past. This gave the United States a foreign service of the first rank in the Western Hemisphere. Futhermore, as an added means of intercommunication, and hence of international friendship, an All-American air service was created.

Another result was the settlement of the Tacna-Arica dispute which had disrupted the relations of Chile and Peru for years. Negotiations had been carried on between these governments and the United States before Hoover took office, and while Frank B. Kellogg was Secretary of State. These were now carried to a successful conclusion and the dispute was settled in accordance with a plan which was developed in the mind of Hoover during his discussions with the governmental officials of these countries at the time of his South American tour. He talked personally with the representatives of Bolivia, Chile and Peru and found out what was in their minds with regard to a proper settlement of the problem. After his return home he suggested to Secretary Stimson, who had succeeded Kellogg, a medial ground upon which all might agree and the solution was accomplished in accordance with his recommendations. All the preliminaries were conducted upon the basis of verbal agreement.

As may be easily understood, the policy of recognition of new governments in Latin America by the United States, offers points of great difficulty. During the Administration of President Hoover two policies were followed. First of all, a general policy, and secondly a special one dealing with Republics of Central America. The general policy followed in granting recognition was explained publicly by Secretary of State Stimson. Before deciding to accord recognition to a newly-established government, there must be satisfactory evidence that this provisional government was *de facto* in control of its country and that there was no active resistance to its rule. Also, the government must make it clear to the United States, that it was its intention to fulfill its international obligations and it was anticipated that, in due course of time, it would hold elections to make its status regular. Aside from the question of the protection of American rights, it was stated clearly, at various times, that it was not the policy of the United States Government to associate its recognition with any particular type of government or political institution which the people of the country in question might decide to adopt. The important question was whether or not the government to be recognized intended and was able to provide adequate protection to foreign rights and fulfill its international obligations. In short, in the matter of recognition of new governments Hoover returned to the traditional policy of the United States of basing recognition on *de facto* control of the country and an ability to fulfill international obligations. This was a change from the policy followed since the time of President Wilson, under which non-recognition was used as a means of interfering in the internal affairs of the smaller Latin-American countries.

With regard to the five Central American Republics, the United States co-operated with those Republics in accordance with the non-recognition policy determined upon in 1923 by the five Republics themselves in a treaty of Peace and Amity. In this treaty it was provided that governments which came into power in any of the five Republics through a coup d'état or revolution against a recognized government should not be recognized "so long as the freely elected representatives of the people thereof have not constitutionally reorganized the country." In addition there were certain restrictions upon the accession to office of head of the State of any person who had held certain designated offices. Furthermore, the United States never attempted to dictate or control the actions of the people of the country concerned. The Hoover Administration thus followed the same policy in Central America as did its predecessors.

Another important policy of the United States Government consisted in its refusal to permit its facilities to be used by any Latin-American Government which was preparing for hostilities.

In his first annual message to Congress, on December 3, 1929, Hoover stated[3] that about 1,600 marines from an expedition of some years before still remained in Nicaragua. This occupation was at the urgent request of the government and leaders of all parties in that country pending the training of a domestic constabulary capable of insuring tranquility. These forces had already been materially reduced but he was anxious to make further withdrawals as the situation might warrant. He added: "In the large sense we do not wish to be represented abroad in such manner." As a proof of his determination to end this intervention, he gave directions to withdraw all marines from Nicaragua and the final withdrawal began on June 3, 1931.[4] This was completed early in January, 1933.

The Republic of Haiti offered a more difficult problem, the solution of which was "still obscure" as Hoover stated in the same message. At that time there were about 700 marines in the island Republic. A few days later, on December 7, 1929, he sent a special message

[3]*State Papers,* Vol. I, p. 140.   [4]Wilbur and Hyde, p. 589.

to Congress requesting that body to authorize an official commission to investigate conditions in Haiti and report when and how we might be able to withdraw. This was granted by Congressional action, and Hoover stated on February 4, 1930,[5] he had no desire for representation of the American Government abroad through our military forces. We had entered Haiti in 1915 for reasons arising from a condition of chaos which was the result of a long period of civil war and disorganization. We had assumed by treaty the obligation to assist the Republic in the restoration of order, the organization of an efficient police force, the rehabilitation of its finances, and the development of its natural resources. In other words, there was the implied obligation to assist in building up a stable self-government. Since then peace and order had been restored and many other of the objectives in general had been attained under the leadership of United States Marine officers. There had been striking economic improvement. Now was the time for the institution of a new and definite policy, looking toward the ending of these treaty relations.

The Haitian Commission, of which W. Cameron Forbes was the chairman, was in the island early in 1930, and confined itself to making recommendations for the future and trying to bring about an agreement between contending Haitian political factions. After protracted negotiations, an accord with the Haitian

[5]Press Conference Statement, *State Papers,* Vol. I, p. 209.

Government was signed by the American Minister, Dana G. Munro, on August 5, 1931, which provided for the return of the majority of the treaty services to Haitian control. In the following year Munro also negotiated a treaty under which all of the American military forces would have been eventually withdrawn and the financial control would have been modified. This treaty was not ratified by the Haitian Congress but it formed the basis of an executive agreement entered into by the Roosevelt Administration in 1933. The final withdrawal of the Marines from Haiti, which was carried out by the Roosevelt Administration, was simply in accordance with plans already worked out under Hoover's direction.

The situation in Cuba was, on account of local politics, one of the most difficult with which the Hoover Administration had to deal. Here, as in other Caribbean countries, the most important aspect of Hoover's policy was the effort to restrict American interference in local political affairs. The withdrawal from Nicaragua and Haiti, the refusal to interfere in the troubled situation in Cuba, the return to the old rule in the matter of recognition of new governments—all formed the basis for a general policy which the Roosevelt Administration has been wise to continue.

During the four years of the Hoover Administration the importance of our economic relations with the Latin-American countries was continued on account of the investments of American citizens in those countries, the greater part of which were made before Hoover took office. Thence arose many problems of great complexity; made especially important by the abandonment of the policy of armed intervention by the United States Government. At this time the holdings by American citizens of bonds issued by the national, state or municipal governments of Latin America approximated a total of a billion dollars. Careful investigation and appraisal of the various local situations were made by representatives of the United States Government and advice and assistance of proper character were given to the interests involved. Also various misunderstandings between our citizens and those of the countries involved were removed from time to time. One of the greatest causes of difficulty was the complicated problem of international exchange following the depression of 1929. In order to protect gold reserves and support their currencies, many of these countries laid prohibitions on the export of gold and stiff restrictions to control not only the rate but also the availability of its exchange. These restrictions frequently were changed with great rapidity, thus increasing the confusion incidental to international trade. It was here that information and advice frequently were given by governmental representatives.

A fair summary of the Latin-American policy of Herbert Hoover was given by him in an address on April 14, 1931, at the celebration of Pan-American

Day.[6] He stressed the fact that his visit in the winter of 1928-9 had made a deep and lasting impression upon him. He added: "It was inspiring to observe, at first hand, not only the progress that Latin America is making along social, economic and cultural lines, but also the important part which the countries . . . are destined to play in world affairs. It was clear, too, that the nations of America have everything to gain by keeping in close touch with one another and by developing that spirit of mutual confidence which has its roots in a reciprocal understanding of national aims and aspirations. Although each of the republics of this hemisphere possesses problems peculiar to itself, there are certain basic questions related to democratic progress and social betterment common to us all and in the solution of which we can be most helpful to one another. This spirit of mutual helpfulness is the cornerstone of true Pan-Americanism."

Hoover stressed the importance of a better acquaintance with the history, the traditions, the culture and the ideals of the other republics of America on the part both of the United States and of the Latin-American nations. According to his view: "A peculiarly heavy responsibility rests upon the nations of the Western Hemisphere; a responsibility which, at the same time, is a high privilege. Richly endowed by nature, we enjoy the great advantage of inhabiting a hemisphere free from the

[6]*State Papers,* Vol. I, pp. 543–545.

jealousies and antagonisms which have proved such obstacles to progress and prosperity in other sections of the world. We have developed an international system based on the principle of equality, combined with a full recognition of the obligations as well as the rights of States. The American republics are today rapidly approaching the time when every major difference existing between them will be settled by the orderly processes of conciliation and arbitration. In this respect, the Western Hemisphere has placed an enviable record before the nations of the world. . . .

"The full significance of this achievement is not always realized, for it carries with it heavy obligations to posterity. Future progress along these lines can only be assured through constant vigilance and by an unswerving determination to make the Union of the American Republics, as now expressed in the Pan American Union, an example to the world. We are not attempting in any way to develop a super-state, or to interfere with the freedom of action of any of the States, members of the Union, but rather to develop an atmosphere of good will—a spirit of co-operation and mutual understanding—in which any difference that may arise, no matter how important, will find a ready solution."

The importance of this address was stressed by Dr. L. S. Rowe, the Director General of the Pan American Union at Washington, D. C., in a personal letter to Hoover under date of May 21, 1931, in which he told the President: "this address has been reproduced in full in practically all the newspapers of Latin America. In many instances, your address, which was sent out in both Spanish and Portugese, was an integral part of the celebrations held in Latin American countries."

The continued stressing by Hoover of the unity of purpose and ideals of the republics of the Western Hemisphere, combined with the abandonment of the policy of intervention, worked a complete and favorable transformation in our relations with the Latin-American states.

The policy of the Hoover Administration was to help and encourage the Latin-American countries in their efforts to achieve autonomy, independence and stability. In contrast to this is the so-called "Good Neighbor" policy of the Roosevelt Administration—a term borrowed from the late Elihu Root, who, as Secretary of State in the Administration of Theodore Roosevelt, first used the term in the year 1907.[7] This policy, taking advantage of the contemporary war situation in Europe, recently seems to have evolved into a "dollar" diplomacy of the type pursued by the Taft Administration of 1909-1913.

[7]P. C. Jessup, *Elihu Root*, Vol. II, p. 563.

IV

NAVAL LIMITATION—THE PRELIMINARIES
THE RAMSAY MacDONALD VISIT

PRESIDENT HARDING had begun the limitation of naval
armaments at the Washington Conference of 1921.
Hoover was a member of the Advisory Committee. This
Conference had limited capital ships quantitatively and
certain other types qualitatively but rival building had
continued in cruisers and other kinds of craft which
make up a large part of the naval tonnage of the great
powers. President Coolidge had attempted to extend
the limitation to these other craft but the Conference
which he had called in the year 1927 had failed. In
1928, both Great Britain and the United States were
drifting towards a serious crisis, but this fortunately
could be met and prevented on account of a change of
administrations in both countries. Now, within a month
after his inauguration, Hoover instructed Ambassador
Hugh Gibson, as his representative, to propose to the
Preparatory Commission for the European Arms Conference a new basis upon which to approach the problem of naval limitation.

Also President Hoover seized the opportunity offered
by his Memorial Day speech at Arlington National
Cemetery to begin a campaign for naval limitation by
asserting that the Kellogg Pact should be supported

by such armament limitations.[1] Said he: "if this agreement is to fulfill its high purpose, we and other nations must accept its consequences; we must clothe faith and idealism with action. That action must march with the inexorable tread of common sense and realism to accomplishment. If this declaration really represents the aspirations of peoples; if this covenant be genuine proof that the world has renounced war as an instrument of national policy, it means at once an abandonment of the aggressive use of arms by every signatory nation and becomes a sincere declaration that all armament hereafter shall be used only for defense."

Hoover continued by making certain proposals of a character specific enough to furnish a program for future negotiations with the great naval powers. Said he:

"But to arrive at any agreement through which we can, marching in company with our brother nations, secure reduction of armament, we must find a rational yardstick with which to make reasonable comparisons of their naval units with ours and thus maintain an agreed relativity. So far the world has failed to find such a yardstick. To say that such a measure cannot be found is the counsel of despair, it is a challenge to the naval authorities of the world, it is the condemnation of the world to the Sisyphean toil of competitive armaments.

[1]Entire address in *State Papers,* Vol. I, pp. 64–68.

"The present Administration of the United States has undertaken to approach this vital problem with a new program. We feel that it is useless for us to talk of the limitation of arms if such limitations are to be set so high as virtually to be an incitement to increase armament. The idea of limitation of arms has served a useful purpose. It made possible conferences in which the facts about national aspirations could be discussed frankly in an atmosphere of friendliness and conciliation. Likewise the facts of the technical problems involved, and the relative values of varying national needs, have been clarified by patient comparison of expert opinions.

"But still the net result has been the building of more fighting ships. Therefore we believe the time has come when we must know whether the pact we have signed is real, whether we are condemned to further and more extensive programs of naval construction. Limitation upward is not now our goal, but actual reduction of existing commitments to lowered levels.

"Such a program, if it be achieved, is fraught with endless blessings. The smaller the armed force of the world, the less will armed force be left in the minds of men as an instrument of national policy. The smaller the armed force of the world, the less will be the number of men withdrawn from the creative and productive labors. Thus we shall relieve the toilers of the nations of the deadening burden of unproductive expenditures,

and above all, we shall deliver them from the greatest
of human calamities—fear. We shall breathe an air
cleared of poison, of destructive thought, and of poten-
tial war."

Hoover now began active personal negotiations with
Prime Minister J. Ramsay MacDonald through Secretary Stimson and Ambassador Charles G. Dawes. He
had learned long ago that the success of all conferences
was built on careful ground work, by competent men,
months in advance of any meeting. At first these were
informal in character, and at times consisted merely in
conversations between MacDonald and Dawes. The
Prime Minister showed himself open-minded to the suggestions of President Hoover and was actuated by a
spirit of frankness and fairness. The fine personal relations between the parties concerned finally resulted,
after several months of negotiation, in a preliminary
basis of agreement which seemed to offer hopeful prospects of a real settlement. This basis consisted of the following general principles: the conversations, as Hoover
earlier had anticipated in his Memorial Day Address,
were to be regarded as the extension of the principles
of the Kellogg Pact. Great Britain disavowed any intention of building up a navy in competition with the
United States. Instead both nations were to accept
parity in the combatant strength of the two navies, and
also the possibility, not only of limitation, but of reduction in naval strength. While the conversations covered

all types of naval armament, yet the main problem to be solved was that of the relative cruiser strength of the navies of the two countries. A tentative agreement was finally reached upon this subject.

The terms of this preliminary agreement were communicated to other governments and were tentatively accepted by Japan but rejected by France and Italy. In spite of this set-back, Hoover determined to proceed with his negotiations. He always has been a strong advocate of personal conference between parties as the best means of settling differences and reaching agreements. He therefore invited Premier MacDonald to visit him at Washington and the latter accepted the invitation. MacDonald also showed his attitude of frankness and warmth of personal regard by letting it be known to Hoover that in determining the time and circumstances of his visit he would be guided entirely by the question of expediency with regard to the present state of negotiations and the convenience of the President. The time was finally decided upon as that of the early part of the month of October, 1929.

Hoover had been in the closest touch with the entire negotiations which were conducted by Secretary Stimson and Ambassador Dawes under his personal direction. From time to time he drew up various summaries of naval construction, tonnage, and armament, especially as applied to cruisers, and was insistent that there should be sufficient agreement between the two countries

to make a definite basis for further negotiations at the
time of MacDonald's visit. On September 7, 1929, he
had written a long letter to Secretary Stimson in which
he summed up at great length and with firm grasp of
the technical matters involved the progress of the negotiations to date. He stated significantly: "I have been
giving a great deal of thought over the week-end to the
Prime Minister's latest dispatches. . . . I dislike the
idea that Mr. MacDonald's visit might become one of
negotiation or split on such a question as this [cruiser
strength] for our whole great program might in the
public mind degenerate into a huckster's quibble; nor
does it seem to me that we should fail to call the conference because of such a gap. The purpose of the conference is to find methods for surmounting difficulties
that we cannot solve otherwise. . . .

"This discussion between our governments has been
in progress now for about three months. There has been
time for public opinion to react on all sides, and there
is the most extraordinary unanimity and prayer
throughout both countries and the whole world that we
shall succeed in actually reducing naval strength, not
that we shall increase it. . . .

"Another still more important phase of the whole
discussion that I think we should bring in, and which
I would appreciate Mr. MacDonald's having in mind,
is whether or not as part of this preliminary accord
we could not settle the proportion of replacements of

battleships we should propose to the January conference that are to be undertaken prior to 1936. . . .

"It would seem to me a most effective and comforting statement if we could arrive at some such proposal as this during Mr. MacDonald's visit and could announce it as part of the conclusion at which we have arrived. Obviously proportionately the same reduction would need be accepted by the other signatories to the Washington agreement and they should be glad to have such an opportunity. I shall look forward to the Prime Minister's visit as an opportunity for most distinguished accomplishment."

While Premier MacDonald was on the high seas the President sent him the following dispatch.

> Washington
> October 3, 1929

Via Radio

The Right Honorable James Ramsay MacDonald, M.P.,
Prime Minister of Great Britain,
    S. S. BERENGARIA.

As you near the shores of the United States I send to you a most cordial welcome not only in my own name but on behalf of my fellow countrymen as well.

> (Signed) Herbert Hoover

The visit of Premier MacDonald was a great success from both the personal and the official standpoints. He was received with friendly acclaim wherever he went. The personal negotiations were conducted by Hoover and MacDonald in large part at the Rapidan Camp in Virginia. Here, in the beautiful mountains of that region, and wandering along the upper reaches of the stream or sitting informally side by side on a log over it, the active heads of two of the greatest world powers discussed as man to man the common problems that were facing them and their respective countries. Both here and at the White House the discussions were frank, friendly and sympathetic. In a recent letter to the author, under date of November 7, 1939, the Rt. Hon. Malcolm MacDonald, son of the late Prime Minister and at the time of writing Secretary of State for the Colonies in the Ministry of Prime Minister Neville Chamberlain, wrote that: "I know how greatly my father enjoyed his visit to Mr. Hoover when he was at the White House, and that it was for him one of the happiest episodes of his public life." On October 9, 1929, the President and Premier finally came to an agreement upon the major questions involved. This was subject to the approval of Japan. They issued a joint statement on October 10, 1929,[2] which was a condensation of several pages of agreement between them written down at the time, the original of which is contained in Mr. Hoover's collection of private papers. Since this statement shows the extent to which Hoover and Mac-

[2]*State Papers*, Vol. I, pp. 107–109.

Donald were able to go in their personal agreement upon matters of policy, it is herewith given.

"During the last few days we have had an opportunity not only to review the conversations on a naval agreement which have been carried on during this summer between representatives of the United States and Great Britain, but also to discuss some of the more immediate obstacles in the way of a vigorous world peace policy. We have been guided by the double hope of settling our own differences on naval matters and so establishing unclouded good-will, candour and confidence between us, and also of contributing something to the solution of a problem in which all other nations are interested and which calls for their co-operation.

"The Paris Peace Pact declares that war has been outlawed and nations have ratified this Pact. Both our Governments resolve to accept the Peace Pact not only as a declaration of good intentions but as an obligation to direct national policy in accordance with its pledge. They are therefore determined to co-operate in creating machinery for the settlement by peaceable means of the disputes which have hitherto led to war.

"The part which each of the governments we represent will have to play will be different, as one will never consent to become entangled in European diplomacy and the other is resolved to pursue a policy of co-operative friendship with its European neighbours; but both in harmony will direct their thoughts and influence toward securing and maintaining the peace of the world.

"Our conversations have been largely confined to the mutual relations of the two countries in the light of the situation created by the signing of the Peace Pact. Therefore, in a new and reinforced sense the two governments not only declare that war between them is unthinkable, but that attitudes and suspicions arising from doubts and fears which may have been justified before the Peace Pact must now cease to influence national policy. We approach old historical problems from a new angle and in a new atmosphere. On the assumption that war between us is banished, and that conflicts between our military or naval forces cannot take place, these problems have changed their meaning and character, and their solution, in ways satisfactory to both countries, has become possible.

"We have agreed that those questions should become the subject of active consideration between us. They involve important technical matters requiring detailed study. One of the hopeful results of the visit which is now terminating officially has been that our two governments will begin conversations upon them following the same method as that which has been pursued during the summer in London."

In the personal discussions with MacDonald an interesting proposal was made by Hoover which has not hitherto been published. It was formulated by him in the following memorandum:

"Army, Navy and Military Aviation Stations

"The General Board of the United States Navy have put their opinion on record that the exisiting military and naval stations of Great Britain in the Western Hemisphere are not in their present condition an appreciable menace to the United States.

"Great Britain will not hereafter establish any military, naval or military aviation stations in her possessions in the Western Hemisphere nor alter any existing stations in such a way as to become a menace to the United States.

"Reciprocally, the United States makes the same agreement as to the Eastern Hemisphere.

"It is understood, however, by both parties that the above declaration does not alter nor supersede the provisions of Article 19 of the Washington Treaty of 1922 for the Limitation of Naval Armament within the territory covered therein.

"The Western Hemisphere is to be defined as that portion of the globe lying West of the 30 meridian and East of the 170 meridian, and the Eastern Hemisphere as the remainder of the globe. This arrangement may be placed in treaty form if it seems desirable."

Hoover made the above definite proposal to Mac-Donald that the United States and Great Britain should agree upon a meridian of longitude which should be a dividing line between their naval stations. This proposal was accepted by MacDonald but the British Ad-

miralty promptly turned it down. Of course on account
of its revolutionary nature with regard to British-Amer-
ican policy this was not included in the press release
of October 10, 1929, mentioned above, which gave a
joint statement by the President and Prime Minister
of the progress and nature of the negotiations. The
matter of immunity of food ships will be discussed in
a subsequent chapter (VI).

Mr. MacDonald left Washington on October 10.
Two days later he sent the following to Hoover:

> "The Weylin
> "54th Street and Madison Avenue
> "New York
> "12 October 1929
>
> "Dear Mr. President
>
> "This is a purely personal letter from guest to host
> to tell you and Mrs. Hoover how vastly well entertained
> were 'the visiting firemen.' I think and feel that with
> help of the local brigade—between us but not entre
> nous—we have done something to insure our citizens
> against conflagrations.
>
> "I am sending this brief note on my birthday and on
> the eve of my departure, and have almost wished my-
> self 'many happy returns'—but must not thus alarm (?)
> you.
>
> "With kindest regards to you both, I am
> "Yours very sincerely
> "(Signed) J. RAMSAY MacDONALD"

65

The correspondence was continued through the following letters which may serve as a convenient introduction to the story of the London Conference on limitation of naval armaments to be told in the following chapter (V).

"October 26, 1929

"My dear Mr. Prime Minister

"I have your very kind note of October 15th. [sic]

"I suppose the visiting fireman upon return to his engine house will find someone who will contend the job could be better done. You can if necessary denounce him upon my authority.

"I have just returned from the Midwest where I have had a week of 10 minute stands so that I can in a measure sympathize with your feelings after a month of it.

"Mrs. Hoover and I both wish to be remembered to Miss MacDonald—and to wish you yourself every success.

"Sincerely,
"(Signed) Herbert Hoover"

"10-Downing Street,
"Whitehall
"19th November, 1929

"My dear President,

"I meant to write to you before this reporting progress, but as you may have seen by the papers I returned

66

to troublesome waters and every hour of my day has been filled by the concerns of my office. To try and arrange the affairs of State is of itself an arduous task, but when every move is watched by imps whose sole purpose is to interfere with evil intent and to plan failure, it becomes almost an impossible one. You know all this, however, and I need say no more.

"According to my promise, a Committee of the Cabinet is now examining the various problems and considerations involved in 'the freedom of the seas' including your own contribution regarding food ships, and the question of fortified bases is referred to a committee of the Committee of Imperial Defence.

"There is practically universal comfort and pleasure here over my visit to you. Immediate results of a detailed kind are not expected but there is happiness that we understand each other with more goodwill. Hesitation is not dispelled and in some quarters it is vocal. When you remember your own difficulties with your Big Navy people you will know to what I refer. If a storm is not to break out to swamp us before we have got the people to apply reason to our work, we must put the issues carefully before the country. As I put it at New York, our people have a deep sentimental regard for their historical position on the sea and however much conditions of to-day demand a reexamination of the position, the simple fact of reexamination is apt to unsettle and stampede them.

"At the Lord Mayor's Banquet a week ago I announced the reexamination to 700 guests gorgeous in uniform and wordly array, representative of interests which are not mine and moved by fears and sentiments which were embodied in the monuments to Nelson and Wellington on the walls, and they took it all right. Several people who must have been shocked to find a Labour Prime Minister the guest of honour for the first time at the Guildhall spoke to me afterwards and, whilst expressing a hope that we should be careful, said they agreed that the question should be examined and be accommodated to the new world. Most of the papers were quite calm on the subject and those which showed concern have no great influence.

"The Navy League, however, is issuing warnings and preparing to be active, some speeches of a hostile character have been delivered, whilst passing across the hall of the United Services Club this week I overheard two officers conversing angrily on the subject, and my First Lord (Mr. Alexander) reports that the Admiralty is fluttering. There is also a certain body of opinion here which is inclined to take the view that the arrangements we are making—parity, etc.—are almost exclusively of the nature of disadvantages to us for which we receive no corresponding advantage. It will take our people some time to understand the argument you put up to us that your foodship proposal was really in our interest. That is the worst I can report. My secretary tells me, however, that there is a keen watchfulness amongst some Conservative sections. When we have had time to consider the question in all its bearings, I shall report the outlook to you.

"I am looking forward to seeing General Dawes some time this week and to hearing his news. I shall also be glad to shake hands with Mr. Stimson, when he comes over.

"Ishbel joins me in sending kindest regards to Mrs. Hoover and yourself. How good both of you were to us (I do not mean officially but as hosts and human beings!) I am,

"Yours, very sincerely,
"(Signed) J. Ramsay MacDonald
"The Hon. Herbert C. Hoover"

"December 3, 1929

"The Honorable
"Ramsay MacDonald
"London, England
"Dear Mr. Prime Minister:

"I have your kind letter of November 19th.

"I have followed with very great interest the reactions both here and in England upon your return. It seems to me that they have all of them advanced the broad issues of better understanding. I have no doubt of the difficulties which confront us both in bringing about a solution in the forthcoming conference. Its success is vital as the next step in all progress.

"We are on our side having some difficulties with those extremists on both sides who disapprove of any kind of an agreement affecting arms. However, the character of the men selected on all sides for the conference in itself gives me great hope.

"Mrs. Hoover joins me in sending compliments of the season to Miss Ishbel and to yourself.

"Yours faithfully,

"(Signed) Herbert Hoover"

V

NAVAL LIMITATION—THE LONDON
CONFERENCE OF 1930

IT HAS always been a basic principle with Herbert Hoover that before deciding upon any matter of importance he should secure authoritative and wide information from every possible source. While his decisions would be his own yet they would be based upon a background of the most reliable facts and information. Following this line of policy, Hoover kept in close touch with the technical experts in the various departments of the Government. Also he kept closely in touch with the discussions and testimony before the Naval Affairs Committee of the United States Senate. Out of this voluminous and often conflicting material he desired to evolve a sound, consistent, and workable policy. Of course, there was wide difference of opinion among his technical advisers. A number of them held that a Conference for final action on reduction of naval armament was not feasible or desirable at that time for certain definite reasons. First of all, they believed that if a non-technical conference were called Hoover was likely to have in all countries the opposition of the naval experts to any conclusions that might be arrived at. This would add greatly to the burden of ratification if it did not result in actual defeat. Furthermore, the experts desired time thoroughly to digest the various technical questions and they insisted that the American naval experts were not ready as yet to present their views in a final form. Also, they feared that Hoover would be leaving the door open to possible criticism for lack of preparation for the conference, which criticism had been leveled at previous conferences.

On the other hand, the experts believed that a preliminary non-technical conference, confined to the determination of certain broad questions of general policy, not only would greatly contribute to the solution of questions but also would formulate more definitely the technical questions to be considered with the aid of these experts.

With regard to the British Government, the first question would be the possibility of an agreement with the United States that there should be parity between the navies of the two countries. A second question would arise as to whether or not the Conference should consider categories of battleships and cruisers only or should also include the whole matter of naval strength. The experts favored the latter.

Another question arose with regard to the other powers. This was, first of all, as to the general ratio to be accepted by the Japanese and secondly, as to the ratio to be accepted by the French and Italians. If it were impossible to secure agreement with regard to these latter, it would also be the determining factor in deciding the question whether or not they should be members of the final Conference and whether or not this Conference should be limited to the United States, Great Britain, and Japan. These and other questions that might arise later, with the technical problems involved, likewise could be clearly defined at a preliminary Conference. After an interval of some months for preparation and consideration, the final Conference could then be called with greatly increased prospects of success, to deal with limited and agreed upon questions. In contrast to this, a hasty movement was likely to bring disaster and prevent ultimate and complete success.

From the British point of view, success was dependent upon the ability of MacDonald to carry with him all his elements of political support. He easily could be defeated if by hasty action and lack of careful preparation he aroused the opposition of the British Admiralty and the large navy advocates.

Hoover had drawn up on June 25, 1929, the following memorandum as a summary of views to that date:

If the British Government is in accord with us . . . then we would suggest that the preliminary consultation should be held by representatives of the five powers to consider the following questions:

1. To enumerate the technical questions which are to be submitted to the experts in development of methods for determining comparative naval strength.

2. To consider whether the ultimate conference shall deal with the whole gamut of naval strength or only with particular categories, such as cruisers. Our desire is that the ultimate conference should discuss the categories covered by the Washington Treaty as well and thus deal with the entire question of combatant ships of all kinds.

3. The question as to whether there shall be actual reduction of present or authorized construction, or merely limitation, which will result in future construction. We feel strongly that the conference must result in reduction and that this can be done equitably amongst nations.

4. The question of relative strength which will meet Japanese needs and also the problems of France and Italy. If it were impossible to secure agreement with France and Italy, this fact, if developed at the consultation, would also probably determine whether they should be members of the final conference or whether it would be limited to the United States, Great Britain, and Japan.

As already stated, Hoover went ahead, during the summer of 1929, with his personal negotiations with Premier MacDonald through Secretary Stimson and Ambassador Dawes. They reached a preliminary basis of negotiation which was communicated to the other governments and was tentatively accepted by Japan but now was rejected by France and Italy. During all this time the representatives of these governments, both in Washington and London, were kept fully informed of the negotiations. France was concerned with the question of security. In the case of Italy, it was the question of expense and prestige, the latter being conditioned upon parity with the French navy.

Although Hoover was checked in his plans by the opposition of France and Italy, he decided to go ahead with them and, as we have seen, he continued his negotiations with Ramsay MacDonald which led up to the American visit of the latter. Meanwhile Hoover had to meet opposition from another source. This opposition arose from powerful shipping and naval interests in the United States under the active leadership of an organization known as the Navy League. This opposition became so bitter that it charged Hoover with "jeopardizing American national security" to an extent that almost amounted to treason. Hoover met this outrageous attack with great astuteness by taking advantage of a lawsuit brought at this time by William B. Shearer against certain ship-building corporations to collect what he alleged was pay due to him for propaganda which he had carried on to prevent naval limitation in the past.

Hoover had quietly caused investigation to be made by various departments of the Government into the personality and activities of this man with the following results. It was established that Shearer had been engaged for four months during the summer, in active propaganda against the proposed agreement for limitation of arms. He delivered three addresses in opposition to naval disarmament on July 17, August 3, and August 25, 1929. Copies of these addresses were submitted in advance to the secretary of a prominent patriotic organization.

Commencing in July, 1929, Shearer began to circularize national patriotic societies with propaganda against the World Court and against naval disarmament. This consisted of articles of an irresponsible and at times virulent character. The general theme was a denunciation of the former Washington Arms Conference, the League of Nations, and the World Court as sinister creations of Europe. A circular letter under date of September 6, 1929, was sent by Shearer to these patriotic societies which urged them to adopt a form resolution that criticized naval disarmament and called upon Congress to defeat any attempts "to force this nation into the League of Nations, the World Court, or any foreign entanglements regardless of any reservations whatever." This letter also contained the following significant statement:

"To reach and educate the masses it requires publicity to combat the sinister propaganda which is being spread throughout the country. The Hearst newspapers advocate a stand for the principles as laid down by the patriotic organizations. It is the purpose of Mr. William Randolph Hearst to use his entire publicity machinery to advocate the building and maintaining of an equal navy to any, and to defeat the World Court issue, or any issue that would put the United States into foreign entanglements.

"The patriotic organizations have, for the first time, the opportunity of wide publications of their expressions and policies on these vital national issues—National Defense and the World Court."

Hoover struck his blow by a press conference statement on September 6, 1929, which included the following[1]: "I have been much interested in the disclosures in respect to the relation of a naval expert [William B. Shearer] who over a month ago filed a complaint in the New York Courts against three important naval shipbuilding corporations for services described in the complaint, in which he acknowledges having received over $50,000 on account. This propagandist has, during the past few years, organized zealous support for increased armament and has been a severe critic of all efforts of our Government to secure international agreement for the reduction of naval arms, which include activities at the Geneva Conference, and opposition to the movement which I have initiated in the past three months. A part of this propaganda has been directed to create international distrust and hate. . . .

[1]*State Papers*, Vol. I, pp. 98–99.

"I have directed the Attorney General to consider what action we can take. Unless the companies can show an entirely different situation from that which is purported in this suit, we are compelled to consider what measures can be proposed to free the country of such influences.

"Every American has the right to express his opinion and to engage in open propaganda if he wishes, but it is obviously against public interest for those who have financial interest in, or may be engaged in contracts for the construction of naval vessels to secretly attempt to influence public opinion or public officials by propaganda in favor of larger armaments and attempt to defeat the efforts of the Government in world limitation of such armaments or to employ persons for such purposes.

"I am making this statement publicly so that there can be no misapprehension of my determination that our present international negotiations shall not be interfered with from such sources and through such methods."

President Hoover followed this statement with another on September 10 in which he said: "The disclosures of interference with and propaganda against the efforts of the Government in its negotiations of international agreement for reduction of naval armament are already so evident as to require that these matters should be gone into to the very bottom." There followed soon after this an investigation by the Senate Committee on

Naval Affairs which resulted in a further discrediting of Shearer and his activities and a repudiation of them all by the corporations which had employed him.

Hoover showed his statemanship by returning to the practice followed by McKinley in the peace negotiations with Spain in 1898. Using Washington as a post of observation and clearing house for reports, he sent abroad a commission composed of experts and including representatives of great influence in the two parties in the United States Senate. While he dominated and directed the negotiations so far as America was concerned, his modesty and reserve prevented his making the mistakes of personal appearance and political partisanship so disastrous in the case of Woodrow Wilson at the Paris Conference of 1918. The Secretary of State, Henry L. Stimson, headed the American delegation. The other members were Secretary of the Navy Charles Francis Adams, Ambassadors Charles G. Dawes and Hugh Gibson, Senators David A. Reed (Republican) of Pennsylvania, and Joseph T. Robinson (Democrat) of Arkansas, Honorable Dwight W. Morrow, and Admiral William D. Pratt.

This delegation left for the London Naval Conference on January 8, 1930. President Hoover had wished them God-speed on the previous day by means of a public statement in which he said in a very serious vein:[2] "The peoples and the governments of the five nations assem-

2*State Papers*, Vol. I, pp. 202–203.

bling at this meeting are sincerely desirous that agreement shall be brought about by which competition in construction of naval arms is brought to an end, and by which actual reduction in naval burdens of the world shall be accomplished. The difficulties of finding a basis that will be acceptable to five different nations are great, but they are not insuperable.

"The conclusions of the Conference must be such as to give a sense of security and satisfaction to each of the nations. Permanent peace is never based on either taking advantage of or accepting a position of prejudice.

"The technology and the complexities of the problems are such that we need hope for no immediate and quick results. To complete the Conference in three or four months would be in itself a great accomplishment, and we should not expect any hurried conclusions. It is the most important of international conferences of a great many years, and probably the most important for many years to come. The progress of peace for the world rests in a great measure upon the shoulders of the five delegations. There is good-will toward the Conference on the part of every nation. The importance and the gravity of the occasion have been recognized in the dispatch to London of the leading men of every country. They have the will to succeed.

"I hope that the people of our country will co-operate in the progress of the Conference by patience, encouragement, and freedom from criticism. We go to London in a fine atmosphere of international good-will, and it is the duty of our country to preserve that atmosphere so far as lies within our power."

The American delegation more than met the expectations of President Hoover and the American people. Their unity of purpose and action, under the leadership of Secretary Stimson, was the main source of strength. Full delegation meetings were held almost daily in order that each member might be fully informed of what was taking place. At these meetings there was a marked spirit of unselfishness, broadness of viewpoint, and a spirit of co-operation.

The Conference lasted for three months with the usual difficulties to meet and overcome, among which were the natural desires of the negotiating countries to secure the most advantageous terms and to relinquish as little as possible. Also there was strong and at times vicious propaganda, both at home and abroad, to influence the course of the negotiations on the part of such diverse interests as the big navy people and imperialists on the one hand and the peace societies and individual pacifists on the other.

It was the French generally who made difficulty in this Naval Conference of 1930. During the month of December they had officially let it be known to Hoover that what they wished particularly to avoid was a repetition of their unfortunate experiences at the Washington Naval Conference in 1921 which evidently they considered to have been detrimental to their interests. They would go to the approaching London Conference with their necessities carefully outlined. What France now desired above all things was that her case be considered on its merits with a careful and sympathetic understanding of her position as a Continental as well as a maritime power. The French delegation now demanded, as the price of their co-operation, a guarantee of security. This idea may have appealed to certain members of the American delegation. President Hoover refused to consider any such undertaking.[3] He was convinced that no matter in what form these assurances were formulated they would be insisted upon as an American obligation in time of war.

Hoover, keeping in close touch with negotiations, on February 27 drew up a memorandum for the information of the various American officials. This memorandum is herewith given in full as illustration of the difficult progress of the work of the Conference.

"I have felt that it was undesirable for me to make any comment either to the Commission or publicly on the progress of negotiations. The general situation, however, as we see it both on this side and from reflection of dispatches as to the attitude of various powers, leads us to make the following comment for your tentative consideration.

"1. We must accept the fact that this country and

3Wilbur and Hyde, p. 592.

the world generally has become pessimistic about the practical results of the conference. This pessimism is based upon:

"*a.* The failure of Mr. MacDonald to carry through further reduction of the British cruiser program as indicated at the Rapidan.

"*b.* Increase in destroyer programs from 150,000-ton basis in our previous negotiations with the British to 200,000 tons, and of submarine from 60,000 to 99,000 tons.

"*c.* The demands of the French, of such character as to upset the British conception of European balance, and likely to further increase British basis and consequently ours beyond your proposal which is already too high, are no doubt put forward with view to securing guarantees either actual or moral, in which we as well as the British should be involved.

"*d.* The demands of the Japanese in respect to the Far East.

"2. These demands of British, Japanese and French drive the conference far from our previous hopes and are only partially compensated for by the proposal that there be 4 American battleships and 6 British battleships actually scrapped and that there should be a holiday in construction of any further battleships until 1936, and even these concessions seem now in doubt in view of pressure from Japan and France.

"3. In view of these situations it strikes me that

"*a*. Of course a 5-power agreement is desirable, but such an agreement if it implied still further expansion in American and British fleets, would be of no value to the world.

"*b*. If the price of preventing this increase in American and British fleets is that we should join in guarantees and contracts for French security, the price is too high to pay.

"4. We are not so much interested in the French fleet except through its effect upon the British and if the British wish to increase the ratio of the French fleet, while it does not make for world peace, it should not be a point on which we should break the conference.

"5. If the British are prepared to make any undertakings of guarantee or assurance to France which do not involve us, we should of course be glad to have their relations settled.

"6. Any notion of our entering into agreements of the type of the Pacific Treaties, or even Presidential interpretation of the Kellogg Pact would unquestionably create great resentment here and dangerously jeopardize the entire agreement.

"7. If a 5-power agreement cannot be obtained without increasing the American base, we suggest for your consideration that you should, even at the price of some concession to the Japanese on cruisers, endeavor to secure a 3-power agreement in which destroyers and submarines should be reduced from 200,000 to 150,000

84

tons and from 99,000 to 60,000 tons with appropriate political agreement protecting the signatories against dangerous and excessive building on the part of other powers.

"I believe that internal economic pressures and world pressures would at least act to prevent France and Italy from exceeding what would be an appropriate fleet prior to 1936.

"8. While we are extremely desirous that the Japanese should not exceed the Washington Treaty ratios, it seems to us that from a naval point of view, the fact that their fleet with a cruiser strength comprise somewhere below 10.7 is not a particularly material thing and that a larger ratio than 10.10 to 10.6 on submarines would not be particularly dangerous as in any event she has an inferior fleet."

It was at this time that Hoover began to feel the full effects of the opposing forces of propaganda and pressure. Starting with certain sections of the American correspondents and apparently with the sympathetic support of M. Briand, there developed, about this time, a definite drive which demanded that Hoover should make a public announcement of policies concerning the Kellogg Pact. The object was to satisfy the French, as already stated, that they might obtain some form of American assurance of political security. This drive now took the form of statements by the European correspondents that the President should save the Conference from disruption and failure by making some sort of pronouncement favorable to the French point of view. The world was given to understand that if the Conference should fail it would be the fault of President Hoover since he had failed to meet French needs by even so moderate an assurance. Hoover also received private advices that such action on his part would satisfy the French.

The constant repetition of the statement that the future of the Conference depended upon the courage of Hoover, that he alone could save the Conference, and that the responsibility for failure would rest upon him, appeared to be primarily a matter of French propaganda. It was designed to see if some form of American political assurance might be secured. In case the Conference should fail it was intended to place responsibility for such failure upon Hoover or upon the United States.

The above propaganda was accompanied in the United States by agitation on the part of American Peace Groups which demanded that the President save the Conference from failure by this action. Hoover steadily ignored these activities and continued with rare wisdom to preserve his equanimity and continue his efforts for a successful and practicable result. There were no real differences of views between him and the American delegation in London. This delegation always had his unqualified support and authority. Hoover was confident that when the other powers had worked out their various problems so as to permit of the success of the great purpose of the Conference, that is to say, the reduction and limitation of naval arms, the United States could be found receptive to full co-operation in preserving the peace of the world. It was his hope and expectation that a plan for accomplishing this could be evolved which would be consonant with the views of the American people and meet their approval as well as that of the Conference. He was confident that the American people gave almost unanimous support to the Briand-Kellogg Pact. But if it was desired that the United States should co-operate in the maintenance of peace, such co-operation must be entirely along the line of improving the machinery of pacific settlement as distinguished from the use of coercive measures of any character. The success of this Conference would be considered by the American people to be a triumph in international co-operation. It would be a proof to them that such co-operation could be undertaken with beneficial results and without any subsequent liabilities.

The type and scope of the propaganda at home may be illustrated by the fact that persons connected with the Foreign Policy Association in New York City received cable advices from London that the American delegation was dissatisfied, that they received no constructive support from the President, and that they felt the latter could save the situation with the French if he would follow the recommendations of the American delegation with regard to a consultative pact. The Foreign Policy Association now proposed to call a general meeting in New York to protest against the actions of the President and the Administration. This presumptuous proposal was promptly sat upon by cooler heads outside.

As a result of this agitation the President made a statement to his Press Conference which was not for quotation or to be attributed to any authority. This was to the effect that "no consultative pact had been proposed to the United States by any of the governments represented at the Conference; that a consultative pact in the terms being advocated by outside groups in the United States would not secure any reduction of tonnage; that foreign governments fully realize the inability of the United States to enter into any form of pact which carried direct or indirect implication of the use of naval forces, and that being put forward by these outside groups, not being of this character, did not meet or assist the situation; that the confidence of these groups that a reduction of tonnage could be secured by the United States offering such a pact was entirely unwarranted."

Among the personal files of Mr. Hoover may be found today the following interesting documents. First of all a copy of a Western Union telegram which reads as follows:

"Washington, D. C., February 25, 1930

"Mr. . . . . ,

. . . . ,

"News reports confirmed by private information indicate London Conference faces grave crisis. Are you willing to join large important group signing following cable to American delegation London. Please telegraph reply to Raymond Fosdick, sixty-one Broadway, New York. Text follows. First upon the reconvening of the Naval Conference we, the undersigned, reiterate the hope that the remaining negotiations be conducted in full remembrance of the fact that all of the powers at London have agreed in the Pact of Paris to renounce war in favor of settling disputes by peaceful means; second, we base our expectations upon President Hoover's Armistice Day Speech in which he declared. Quote: We will reduce our Naval strength in proportion to any other. Having said that it only remains for the others to say how low they will go, it cannot be too low for us. Unquote. This policy of reduction has had and continues to have the overwhelming endorsement and support of the American people. We protest against any possibility that this policy of reduction may be abandoned; third, as a fundamental basis for the reduction of Armaments we urge the importance of taking steps at the London Conference to utilize the principle of joint conference in the case of disputes which otherwise might lead to war; fourth, we pledge to the President and American Delegation our active and continued support for the conclusion of such agreements as embody the principles of reduction and conference and at the same time meet the justly aroused expectations of the entire world. We cannot impress too strongly upon the American delegation the calamitous effect which the failure of the London Conference to achieve these principles would have upon American opinion. Signed Raymond B. Fosdick, James T. Shotwell, Mrs. Carrie Chapman [Catt], Capt. James G. McDonald.

Unsigned"

The second document is as follows:

"*Copy*

"DAY LETTER

". . . .   .

"February 20, 1930

"Raymond Fosdick
61 Broadway
New York, New York

"Since American Delegation in London is an official one representing this nation, acting under instructions from the President of the United States, don't you feel that any expressions of opinions of American citizens should go to the State Department or to the President . . . ?

. . . ."

Early in April, 1930, a treaty was finally assured. Hoover at once recognized this officially by a statement

at a Press Conference on April 11 which was in part
as follows:[4]

"I am greatly pleased with the final success of the
Naval Arms Conference in London and I have today
telegraphed the delegation expressing my approval of
the result achieved and my admiration for their patience
and determination in an arduous and difficult negotiation. And I wish to congratulate the delegations of the
other governments for their constructive and courageous action.

"The most vital feature of its great accomplishments
for peace is the final abolition of competition in naval
arms between the greatest naval powers and the burial
of the fears and suspicions which have been the constant
product of rival warship construction. . . .

"When I initiated this negotiation it was after a
critical examination of the experience before and after
the Geneva Conference and a determination that the
causes of that failure could be met with adequate preparation and preliminary negotiation. At that time we
realized, and have realized at all times since, that the
particular setting of the continental nations, because of
the inseparable importance of land armies in their bearing upon naval strength, together with the political
agreements that reduction of such arms implied, made
a five-power agreement extremely improbable, as the
United States could not involve itself in such agree-

[4]*State Papers*, Vol. I, pp. 230–233.

ments. The French and Italian governments have shown the utmost good will in this conference in endeavor, in the interest of world peace, to support the present solution just as far as they could do so, and they joined the present agreement in important provisions. . . .

"The savings are not alone to the United States but to Great Britain and Japan as well. The total saving to the world is perhaps $2,500,000,000 below the Geneva basis to which the world was steadily drifting. This sum devoted to reproductive enterprise will be a great stimulus to world prosperity.

"There are no political undertakings of any kind in the present treaty except an agreement for the regulation of the conduct of submarines against merchant ships in time of war. The whole agreement is a great step in world peace and an assurance of American parity in naval strength."

The preliminary text of the London Naval Treaty was received by Hoover on April 18, 1930, and a corrected draft during the next three days (April 19-April 21). The Treaty was signed in London on April 22 and Ambassador Dawes sent the following cablegram to President Hoover:

"The treaty has just been signed. The high purpose so near to your heart, the statement of which initiated these negotiations in which you have had such a commanding part is thus translated into an enduring benefit to the world and its peace. The able and courageous

leadership of Stimson has at all times united, coordi-
nated and stimulated the activities of your delegates
here and he and those of the delegation who sail tomorrow have won the general respect and sincere regards
of all with whom they have negotiated. I send my congratulations.

Charles G. Dawes"

Hoover immediately replied as follows:

"Hon. Charles G. Dawes,
American Ambassador to England,
London, England.
"My dear Ambassador:

I have your kind telegram of April 22. I wish to
take this occasion to express to you the deep appreciation I have for the foundations laid by you, which have
contributed so much to make possible the successful
issue of the London conference. I am still uncertain as
to whether we will need your great influence to secure
its ratification by the Senate.

Yours faithfully,
Herbert Hoover"

Hoover was now faced with the problem of securing
ratification, if possible, by the United States Senate.
He was well aware of the forces of opposition he must
meet and began to work toward creating a favorable
public opinion. A supporting newspaper press was one
of the first considerations, so he took advantage of the

presence of the leading journalists of Washington and the country at a dinner of the Gridiron Club on April 26 to make plain the principles and objectives underlying his foreign policies. In the course of his address[5] on this occasion he stated that on a recent occasion where, as President of the United States he was a guest, two eminent foreign journalists had referred to the delinquencies of American foreign policies and the shortcomings of some of our statesmen. In biting terms of justifiable resentment Hoover expressed the hope that whenever American journalists might speak upon occasions where Chief Executives of foreign countries were guests the journalists should neither attack the policies of other nations nor make reflections upon the leading men of their country. It was well for them to remember that the office of a Chief Executive is a symbol of the majesty of a nation and that its leaders should have solidarity in the presence of a foreign attack although they might differ in domestic policies.

Cleverly using this as an introduction, he then stated: "that occasion . . . gave rise in my mind to a thought which, it seems to me, is worthy of elaboration, that is, the higher purpose of our immediate foreign policy. During the Great War the United States demonstrated not only our colossal reserve of military strength, but also an ability quickly to organize it and the valor to use it. The disturbed condition of the world has made

[5]Full text of the address in *State Papers*, Vol. I, pp. 267–272.

it necessary to increase our military strength beyond the peace basis which we maintained before the war, both in naval and land arms. . . . As a result of these forces, a large part of the world had come to believe that they were in the presence of the birth of a new imperial power intent upon dominating the destinies and freedom of other peoples. . . . But it was an utter misconception of America. We know there is neither financial, territorial, nor military imperialism in the American heart. We know that such ideas are anathema to the American mind, and no man could be elected a county commissioner on such a platform. . . . But, rightly or wrongly, there sprung from the spread of these ideas abroad the most dangerous of all international currents—fear. There began to pervade the world a jealousy, a suspicion, and an ill will toward the United States such as never before existed in peace history. Therefore, it became the first duty of . . . the Government to realign this sentiment and this public opinion in the world back to the true actualities of American aspirations. . . .

"We were faced with the great intangible of human relations—that is, human fear and human emotion. The undertaking to revise world misunderstanding could not be founded upon words or preachments, it must be founded upon action. It must comprise itself of the building of a mosaic of deeds which creates a vivid picture of the United States in its true setting to people abroad. If you will review the recent incidents in our foreign relations I hope you will realize that a series of actions has been part of a pattern consciously and progressively directed to this high end. . . .

"Through all this we have, I believe, created a new atmosphere of confidence in our willingness properly to coöperate in solution of world problems. At the same time we have not hesitated to emphasize the fact that the United States will not involve itself in any political agreement which commits it to the use of coercion upon other nations. In our position of transcendent power the very association in military and other coercive measures would dim the picture of our pacific intentions. We have emphasized the American position of independence clear and clean. The United States, devoted to peace, will make its own political policies."

President Hoover submitted the Treaty to the Senate on May 1, 1930.[6] Although the Treaty contained a compromise which resulted in cruiser parity of the American and British fleets on a fair basis, opposition immediately showed itself. The Senate not only delayed moving toward ratification, but also let it be known that it proposed to adjourn without doing so. Furthermore, several members joined in a "round robin" in which they demanded that the President delay ratification. Hoover's reply to this challenge was the announcement

[6]Message of submission and full text of the treaty may be found in *State Papers*, Vol. I, pp. 274–289.

that he would call a special session of the Senate to meet on July 7 for the consideration of ratification.

Meanwhile the following exchange of letters had taken place between Hoover and Ramsay MacDonald.

"1 May 1930
10, Downing Street
Whitehall.

"My dear President

"Before everything relating to our meeting last year has been tied up and pigeonholed, I should like to give you a goodbye. Unfinished work has still to be carried on, but what can be done for the moment has been done and is ready for judgment. We have all done our best to make the Conference a success, and though success has not been complete, it has been substantial.

"You sent over a splendid team who, severally and collectively, contributed very much indeed to what success the Conference had. It is not easy for me to convey to you how much good they really did. They were far more than delegates to a Conference, doing the work of a Conference; they were Ambassadors from one people to another, and the personal loss which we felt when they left was very keen. They will tell you all about the business done and I shall not poach upon their preserves.

"It has been such a pleasure to me to co-operate with you in this work. The mentalities of Europe will mean

97

much negotiation and persuading on our part yet, but we shall go on as best we can.

"The world is not a very pleasant place to try and govern at the present moment, but I hope your difficulties melt before you.

"With my kindest regards and best wishes to Mrs. Hoover (who, I hope, is now quite recovered from her accident) and yourself

> I am, my dear President
> Yours very sincerely,
> J. Ramsay MacDonald"

Hoover promptly replied as follows:

> "May 14, 1930

"My dear Mr. Prime Minister:

"I wish to thank you for your kind note.

"The world makes its progress in short steps, and always by compromise; it is disheartening at times, but the main thing is to keep the light ahead. I do feel that we have laid foundations upon which we or others can build more greatly in times to come.

"I deeply appreciate your kind reference to our delegation. I know that they and I feel deeply the earnest cooperation they received from you and yours.

> "Sincerely,
> "Herbert Hoover"

In view of Hoover's frank statement that he would call the Senate in special session, the opposition to the

treaty not only continued but grew in volume. Among
the public at large there was a fear, carefully fostered,
that the London Naval Treaty had failed to attain
parity between the fleets of Great Britain and the
United States. Hoover issued a press statement on June
13 in defense of the treaty and specifically answering
these objections.[7] Furthermore, Senator George H.
Moses, a leading Republican Senator, wrote Hoover on
June 24 enclosing the request of a number of Senators
that the proposed extra session of the Senate be deferred
until November. Hoover replied that he realized fully
the great strain which had been placed upon the Senate
by the recent long continued session. On the other hand,
he felt that the national interest in having the Naval
Treaty brought to a conclusion was so great that he
must ask that the matter be dealt with at the earliest
possible date. On July 3, the day upon which Congress
adjourned its regular session, a proclamation was issued
formally convening the Senate to meet in special session
four days later.

The Senate duly met on July 7 and on that day
Hoover sent to that body a message in which he carefully summed up the provisions of the treaty and his
reasons for urging its ratification.[8]

"In requesting the Senate to convene in session for
the special purpose of dealing with the treaty for the

[7]*State Papers*, Vol. I, pp. 311–312.
[8]Full text in *State Papers*, Vol. I, pp. 351–356.

limitation and reduction of naval armament signed at London April 22, 1930, it is desirable that I should present my views upon it. This is especially necessary because of misinformation and misrepresentation which have been widespread by those who in reality are opposed to all limitation and reduction in naval arms. We must naturally expect opposition from those groups who believe in unrestricted military strength as an objective of the American Nation. Indeed, we find the same type of minds in Great Britain and Japan in parallel opposition to this treaty. Nevertheless, I am convinced that the overwhelming majority of the American people are opposed to the conception of these groups. Our people believe that military strength should be held in conformity with the sole purpose of national defense; they earnestly desire real progress in limitation and reduction of naval arms of the world, and their aspiration is for abolition of competition in the building of arms as a step toward world peace. Such a result can be obtained in no other way than by international agreement.

"The present treaty is one which holds these safeguards and advances these ideals. Its ratification is in the interest of the United States. It is fair to the other participating nations. It promotes the cause of good relations.

"The only alternative to this treaty is the competitive building of navies with all its flow of suspicion, hate, ill-will and ultimate disaster. History supports those who hold to agreement as the path to peace. Every naval limitation treaty with which we are familiar, from the Rush-Bagot agreement of 1817, limiting vessels of war on the Great Lakes, to the Washington Arms Treaty of 1921, has resulted in a marked growth of good-will and confidence between the nations which were parties to it.

"It is folly to think that because we are the richest nation in the world we can outbuild all other countries. Other nations will make any sacrifice to maintain their instruments of defense against us, and we shall eventually reap in their hostility and ill-will the full measure of the additional burden which we may thus impose upon them. The very entry of the United States into such courses as this would invite the consolidation of the rest of the world against us and bring our peace and independence into jeopardy. We have only to look at the state of Europe in 1914 to find ample evidence of the futility and danger of competition in arms. . . .

"Defense is the primary function of government, and therefore our first concern in examination of any act of this character is the test of its adequacy in defense. No critic has yet asserted that with the navies provided in this agreement together with our army, our aerial defense and our national resources, we cannot defend ourselves, and certainly we want no military establishment for the purpose of domination of other nations.

Our naval defense position under this treaty is the more clear if we examine our present naval strength in comparison to the present strength of the other nations, and then examine the improvements in this proportion which will result from this treaty. This improvement arises from the anticipation of the parity in battleships to be reached ten years hence under the Washington Arms Treaty and the fact that other nations have been building in the classes of ships not limited by that treaty, while we, until lately, lagged behind. . . .

"The more selfish-minded will give little credence to the argument that savings by other parties to the agreement in the limitation of naval construction are of interest to the American people, yet the fundamental economic fact is that if the resources of these other nations are freed for devotion to the welfare of their people and to pacific purposes of reproductive commerce, they will result in blessings to the world, including ourselves. If we were to accept the Geneva Conference base as the end of naval strength under competitive building for the three governments, the saving in construction and operation by the treaty is literally billions of dollars.

"The question before us now is not whether we shall have a treaty with either three more 8-inch cruisers or four less 6-inch cruisers, or whether we shall have a larger reduction in tonnage. It is whether we shall have this treaty or no treaty. It is a question as to whether we shall move strongly toward limitation and reduction in naval arms or whether we shall have no limitation or reduction and shall enter upon a disastrous period of competitive armament.

"This treaty does mark an important step in disarmament and in world peace. It is important for many reasons that it should be dealt with at once. The subject has been under discussion since the Geneva Conference three years ago. The lines of this treaty have been known and under discussion since last summer. The actual document has been before the American people and before the Senate for nearly three months. It has been favorably reported by the Senate Foreign Relations Committee. Every solitary fact which affects judgment upon the treaty is known, and the document itself comprises the sole obligation of the United States. If we fail now the world will be again plunged backward from its progress toward peace."

As stated by Hoover, the Senate Foreign Relations Committee had given careful scrutiny to the Treaty and then favorably reported it. It was during the hearings held by this Committee, that the full benefits were realized from Hoover's wise action in including Senators David A. Reed and Joseph T. Robinson, Republican and Democratic leaders respectively, in his appointments to the American delegation at London. In large measure, and due to their influence, the discussion of the Treaty was almost entirely without regard to party politics. Especially did Senator Reed perform striking service, both in grilling opponents who were actuated more by selfishness than by patriotism, and by showing up the narrowness and unfairness of certain naval experts and bureaucrats. These latter, at times, seemed intent upon impugning the honesty and patriotism of President Hoover. Among other things they attempted to arouse prejudice by charging secret dealings and agreements of an un-American character. A resolution (Senate No. 320) was passed asking Hoover, if not incompatible with public interest, to submit to the Senate "all letters, cablegrams, minutes, memoranda, instructions and despatches, and all records, files and other information touching the negotiations of the London Naval Treaty." On July 11 Hoover promptly sent a message to the Senate in which he refused to submit this confidential material. In this message he stated,[9] in no uncertain terms, that this treaty, like all other international negotiations, "has involved statements, reports, tentative and informal proposals as to subjects, persons and governments given to me in confidence. The Executive, under the duty of guarding the interests of the United States, in the protection of future negotiations, and in maintaining relations of amity with other nations, must not allow himself to become guilty of a breach of trust by betrayal of these confidences. He must not affront representatives of other nations, and

[9] *State Papers*, Vol. I, pp. 357–358.

thus make future dealings with those nations more difficult and less frank. To make public in debate or in the
press such confidences would violate the invariable practice of nations. It would close to the United States those
avenues of information which are essential for future
negotiations and amicable intercourse with the nations
of the world. I am sure the Senate does not wish me to
commit such a breach of trust.

"I have no desire to withhold from the Senate any
information having even the remotest bearing upon the
negotiation of the Treaty. No Senator has been refused
an opportunity to see the confidential material referred
to, provided only he will agree to receive and hold the
same in the confidence in which it has been received and
held by the Executive. A number of Senators have
availed themselves of this opportunity. I believe that no
Senator can read these documents without agreeing
with me that no other course than to insist upon the
maintenance of such confidence is possible."

Hoover now took advantage of his opportunity to
strike a blow directly at those who were attempting to
impugn his frankness and integrity by repeating "with
the utmost emphasis that in these negotiations there
were no secret or concealed understandings, promises or
interpretations, nor any commitments whatever except
as appear in the Treaty itself and in the interpretive
exchange of notes recently suggested by your Committee on Foreign Affairs, all of which are now in the hands

of the Senate." In conclusion he added: "In view of this, I believe that to further comply with the above Resolution would be incompatable with the public interest."

After the usual wrangle had taken place in the Senate, the Treaty was ratified on July 21 by the vote of 58 to 9, and signed on July 22, 1930. Simultaneously, Hoover made the public statement with deep feeling and gratification from the success of his efforts that: "With the ratification by the other governments the Treaty will translate an emotion deep in the hearts of millions of men and women into a practical fact of government and international relations. It will renew again the faith of the world in the moral forces of good will and patient negotiation as against the blind forces of suspicion and competitive armament. It will secure the full defense of the United States. It will mark a further long step toward lifting the burden of militarism from the backs of mankind and to speed the march forward of world peace. It will lay the foundations upon which further constructive reduction of world arms may be accomplished in the future. We should by this act of willingness to join with others in limiting armament, have dismissed from the mind of the world any notion that the United States entertains ideas of aggression, imperial power or exploitation of foreign nations."

Thus, without in any way endangering the national defenses or safety of the United States, Hoover accomplished a substantial naval limitation. During the four years of his Administration the navy was maintained at an average yearly cost of about $350,000,000. In the four years, 1933-1937, before any specific or immediate danger arose,.the annual cost of the navy was increased, under the Roosevelt Administration, to more than $650,000,000.[10]

As a final comment upon and closing of the discussion in this chapter, may be quoted the following letter written in long-hand by the British Prime Minister:

"10, Downing Street
Whitehall.
25 July 1930

"My dear Mr. President

"May I express to you my congratulations and thankfulness at the splendid result of the Senate vote on the Naval Treaty? It fills me with comfort. We have made a beginning but only a beginning, and I pray that those who are in authority in 1935 may take another long stride towards the goal to which we have set our steps. I have the necessary preliminary legislation far advanced here & it will go through next week, & instructions have been given to prepare the documents for ratification. So I shall not be far behind you. I have only held my hand to let you in first.

"The position with France & Italy is not very good yet but we are encouraging it to progress, so far as we may, in the right direction. But the world is hard &

[10]Wilbur and Hyde, p. 597.

107

its burdens are heavy. I am very weary. On Thursday I go to Oberammergau to see the Passion Play once more. Thirty years ago I saw it with my wife & now I take my three girls with me. Time & things pass & we too go.

"I hope that all the best will attend Mrs. Hoover & yourself & believe me to be

"Yours always sincerely

"J. Ramsay MacDonald"

VI

IMMUNITY OF FOOD SHIPS
IN TIME OF WAR

HERBERT HOOVER always has been a practical humanitarian. Realism has been a guiding principle throughout his public life. This cannot be too often repeated. Also his experiences during the World War, as head of Belgian Relief and later as director of relief to the other war-torn peoples of Europe, have created a basis for many of his subsequent plans for human relief. Among these is his belief in, and advocacy of, the principle that food ships should have immunity in time of war. Very recently in an article written during 1939,[1] Hoover drew from his burning memories of the past, and made the following statement:

"And there were the terrors of the air. In a score of air raids I saw the terror of women and children flocking to the cellars, frantically, to escape from an unseen enemy.

"In another even more dreadful sense I saw inhuman policies of war. That was the determination on both sides to bring subjection by starvation. The food block-

[1] "Shall We Send Our Youth to War?" *The American Magazine,* August, 1939.

ade by the Allied Governments on the one side, and the ruthless submarine warfare by the Central Powers on the other, had this as its major purpose. Both sides professed that it was not their purpose to starve women and children. But it is an idiot who thinks soldiers ever starve. It was women and children who died of starvation. It was they who died of the disease which came from short food supplies, not in hundreds of thousands, but in millions.

"And after the Armistice came famine and pestilence, in which millions perished and other millions grew up stunted in mind and body. That is war. Let us not forget."

It has already been shown (Chapter I) that after the Armistice had been signed and the ill-fated Treaty of Versailles was in process of formation, Hoover's main idea was to get food to these starving people of Europe. As early as May 14, 1919, he wrote in Paris to President Wilson a personal letter in which he urged his "strong view that we should not be led into joining with the Allies in a food blockade against Germany as a method of forcing peace." He gave it as his own belief that he seriously doubted "whether when the world has recovered its moral equilibrium that it would consider a peace obtained upon such a device as the starving of women and children as being binding upon the German people." Furthermore, he believed that under the new Wheat Act the United States Government could sell bread stuff to Germany on credit. He added: "this would probably involve acrimonious feeling in the United States for a time, of which I am prepared to stand my full share should it come to this issue."

During subsequent years, while serving as Secretary of Commerce in the Cabinet of President Coolidge, Hoover evolved his theory of uniting the immunity of food ships with measures for national defense. The following letter shows the germ of the constructive plan which was formulating in his mind:

"November 21, 1927

"The President
The White House
Washington, D. C.
"Dear Mr. President:

"I have given further consideration to our discussion as to the method of strengthening the private merchant marine as a measure of defense.

"The suggestion I made was that the Navy Department should offer to enlist all officers and men of the Merchant Marine in a naval reserve, paying salaries and wages to the reserve men on a scale approximated to the difference in wages between foreign vessels and our own. It was also my suggestion that the matter be undertaken entirely as one of defense and budgeting and handling of payments be made from the Navy budget; that this enlistment should be limited to vessels of cargo liner type of a minimum of 10,000 tons and a

minimum of 14 knots speed, and should be applied only
to vessels engaged in regular service on essential trade
routes.

"We find that the total cost would be something
under ten million dollars per annum, that the payment
would amount to about 11 per cent of the present gross
revenues and would apparently make the difference between profit and loss for most of our trade routes. I
believe it would result in replacement, new vessel construction and expansion of service sufficient to cover the
defense needs. It should materially strengthen the navy
personnel if it were organized on a sound basis and
economies might be made in other forms of naval reserve, or perhaps actual naval personnel that would
partially compensate. Its incidental advantages to commerce require no amplification.

"I send you herewith a memorandum covering some
of the data and if you think it worth pursuing the matter further I would suggest that it should be referred
to the Navy Department for an opinion.

"Yours faithfully
(Signed) "Herbert Hoover"

Hoover's real opportunity came two years later at
the time of his personal conference with Prime Minister
Ramsay MacDonald at the Rapidan Camp. In the formal statement which was drawn up and issued to the
public on October 10, 1929, the already-quoted original
document contained a statement which was never pub-

lished. We shall find that Hoover used another opportunity a month later to get his views before the people on the embarrassing complications.[2]

This occasion was his Armistice Day address which possibly may prove to have been one of the most important of his career. It was delivered at the Washington Auditorium, Washington, D. C., on November 11, 1929. In the course of his prepared address, he made the following pregnant statement:[3]

"From the war we have two paramount obligations. We owe to those who suffered and yet lived an obligation of national assistance, each according to his need. We owe it to the dead that we redeem our promise that their sacrifice would help bring peace to the world. The Nation will discharge its obligations.

"The men who fought know the real meaning and dreadfulness of war. No man came from that furnace a swash-buckling militarist. Those who saw its realities and its backwash in the sacrifice of women and children are not the men who glorify war. They are the men who pray for peace for their children. But they rightly demand that peace be had without the sacrifice of our independence or of those principles of justice without which civilization must fail.

"Such a sacrifice of freedom and justice is the one calamity greater than war. The task of statesmen is to build a road to peace which avoids both of these calam-

[2]See Chapter IV for full text of the statement.
[3]*State Papers*, Vol. I, pp. 125–132.

ities. This road requires preparedness for defense; it equally requires preparedness for peace. . . .

"I am for adequate preparedness as a guaranty that no foreign soldier shall ever step upon the soil of our country. . . .

"There is another of these age-old controversies which stir men's minds and their fears. That is the so-called freedom of the seas. In reality in our day it is simply the rights of private citizens to trade in time of war, for there is today complete freedom of the seas in times of peace. If the world succeeds in establishing peaceful methods of settlement of controversies, the whole question of trading rights in time of war becomes a purely academic discussion. Peace is its final solution.

"But I am going to have the temerity to put forward an idea which might break through the involved legal questions and age-old interpretations of right and wrong by a practical step which would solve a large part of the intrinsic problem. It would act as a preventive as well as a limitation of war. I offer it only for the consideration of the world. I have not made it a governmental proposition to any nation and do not do so now. I know that any wide departure from accepted ideas requires long and searching examination. No idea can be perfected except upon the anvil of debate. This is not a proposition for the forthcoming naval conference, as that session is for a definite purpose, and this proposal will not be injected into it.

"For many years, and born of a poignant personal experience, I have held that food ships should be made free of any interference in times of war. I would place all vessels laden solely with food supplies on the same footing as hospital ships. The time has come when we should remove starvation of women and children from the weapons of warfare.

"The rapid growth of industrial civilization during the past half century has created in many countries populations far in excess of their domestic food supply and thus steadily weakened their natural defenses. As a consequence, protection for overseas or imported supplies has been one of the most impelling causes of increasing naval armaments and military alliances. Again, in countries which produce surplus food their economic stability is also to a considerable degree dependent upon keeping open the avenues of their trade in the export of such surplus, and this again stimulates armament on their part to protect such outlets.

"Thus the fear of an interruption in sea-borne food supplies has powerfully tended toward naval development in both importing and exporting nations. In all important wars of recent years, to cut off or to protect such supplies has formed a large element in the strategy of all combatants. We cannot condemn any one nation; almost all who have been engaged in war have participated in it. The world must sooner or later recognize this as one of the underlying causes of its armed situation, but, far beyond this, starvation should be rejected among the weapons of warfare.

"To those who doubt the practicability of the idea, and who insist that agreements are futile for the purpose of controlling conduct in war, I may point out that the Belgian Relief Commission delivered more than two thousand shiploads of food through two rings of blockade and did it under neutral guarantees continuously during the whole World War. The protection of food movements in time of war would constitute a most important contribution to the rights of all parties, whether neutrals or belligerents, and would greatly tend toward lessening the pressure for naval strength. Foodstuffs comprise about 25 per cent of the commerce of the world but would constitute a much more important portion of the trade likely to be interfered with by a blockade."

This proposal for immunity of food ships was greeted with approval both at home and abroad. In the United States it received very wide-spread endorsement from such differing organizations as the Women's Club of Milwaukee, Wisconsin, the Peace Society of Twin Falls, Idaho, and the Ninth Congressional District Republican Club of Long Beach, California. It received special notice in such newspapers as the *Chicago Daily News*, the *Indianapolis Star*, the *Columbia* (S. C.) *State*, also papers in Wheeling, West Virginia, Lincoln, Nebraska and many others. Among individual endorsements were those of Dr. L. S. Rowe, Director General of the Pan-American Union; Dr. H. J. Peterson, of the University of Wyoming; Lewis Stuyvesant Chanler, of the Historical Society of New York City, and the brilliant writer, R. H. Edmonds, Editor of the *Manufacturer's Record* of Baltimore, Maryland.

Hoover also received the following letter of personal endorsement from the Democratic leader of the Senate:

"UNITED STATES SENATE
Conference of the Minority
Little Rock, Arkansas
November 14, 1929

"My dear Mr. President:

"It is my mature conviction that in your *Armistice Day* address is contained a suggestion which will greatly stimulate the movement for permanent International Peace and indirectly facilitate the reduction of armaments. After thinking over the matter for two or three days there appears to be no sound argument which can be urged against the change which you suggest, namely; immunity to food carrying ships from seizure and attack during War. There exists no occasion to ask your attention to any analysis of the subject which I am able to submit. Nevertheless, I claim the privilege of commending your proposal.

"With personal regards, I am

Very truly,
(Signed) "Joe T. Robinson"

"To the President
The White House
Washington, D. C."

The Hoover proposal also was received with welcome by all the South American States, by the European neutrals, and by Germany, Italy, Austria, China, and Japan. Opposition, however, came from Great Britain and France. The British Admiralty quietly squelched the proposal in Great Britain.[4] There was some support there among the Liberals. Gilbert Murray may be quoted as saying of the proposal: "It is demanded by the conscience of the world."

The reception in France was more hostile. While one commentator said, that "the proposal is bound to be condemned by diplomats as unspeakably humane," the French press was outspokenly hostile. The general basis of opposition was upon the grounds that Hoover's suggestion, if adopted, would deprive the League of Nations of one of its chief weapons against an aggressor nation, that is to say, an economic blockade. Also, it was held that a nation engaged in war, if relieved of all worry with regard to the feeding of its people, might have an added inducement to continue the struggle. Finally, French opinion was to the effect that Great Britain can make sure its supply of food only by means of the domination of the seas. Therefore, it was hardly to be expected that the British would give up such pro-

4Wilbur and Hyde, p. 599.

118

tection in exchange for an agreement, or international understanding, that would be dependent for its enforcement or observance upon the force of public opinion and good faith. This was especially true since such means of sanction might be violated under stress of necessity in a time of war.

When Hoover thus found that his proposal for the immunity of food ships had no present prospect of acceptance, he dropped it for a while with the intention of reviving the project whenever opportunity again should offer.

NOTE

This same project of securing immunity of food ships in time of war, has been a matter of great importance in the mind of Herbert Hoover in the years since his retirement from the Presidency in 1933. He foresaw the critical events arising during the summer of 1939 which finally culminated in the war declarations of Great Britain and France, against Germany. He again returned to the subject in a public address delivered in Cleveland, Ohio, on July 6, 1939, before the international convention of Christian Endeavor Societies. In the course of that address he said:

"My proposal is that all nations who are willing to do so should enter an agreement.

"1. That vessels laden solely with food supplies should be placed upon the same basis of immunity as hospital ships. They should go freely. Blockade should not apply to them. There should be no attack upon their passage by either warships or submarines.

"2. That there shall be no bombing of civil populations and no bombing anywhere except in the field of actual fighting men on land or sea, and at works devoted strictly to munitions.

"Nations who are not willing to enter such obligation will have at least declared their shameful devotion to barbarism. They will be proved outcasts from civilization.

"There is humanity in the peoples of all combatant nationalities. Their own public opinion is shocked by barbarities. That is evidenced by the fact that all statesmen in the last war sought to justify such acts to their people as reprisals for the barbarities of the enemy. And through all discussion of preparedness today they find justification in their fears of this frightfulness against themselves.

"Now for the moral teeth that I propose for enforcement. That is the definite participation of neutrals of the world in protection against these barbarities. As a part of such agreement the neutral nations should become the referees announcing in authoritative way any fouls that take place.

"To effect this, such agreement should provide further:

"3. That the shipment of food supplies in war to any

blockaded nation may be in full cargoes under the management and jurisdiction of a commission of the neutral nations.

"4. That neutral observers should be continuously in session within every belligerent country to determine the facts of any killing of civilians from the air.

"The whole of this enforcement by neutrals must be based upon moral forces and not on military force or entanglement in the controversy. Should any belligerent be convicted of deliberate violations, then neutrals should withdraw. Awful as it may be, no doubt the hells of reprisals from the injured side would then be turned loose.

"The real teeth behind this enforcement is public opinion among neutrals. That is one of the most potent forces in modern war. If it be pointed up by definite conviction beyond all the whitewashing of propaganda it can be far-reaching in its consequences.

"In the strategy of modern war one of the utmost anxieties of both sides is to hold the good will of neutrals. Or at least to prevent their indignation forcing them to aid or to join the enemy. The ill will of neutrals or their citizens at once induces informal boycotts of credit and supplies, even do they go no further. To influence neutral public opinion in the last war every combatant spent millions in gigantic propaganda. And they are spending it again today.

"Public opinion in neutral nations does not react

much to the legalistic question of whether cotton is contraband or non-contraband. It does not react much to imperial ambitions of combatants. It does not react much to specious circumventions of such instruments as the Kellogg Pact. But it does react to the horror of killing women and children.

"It is asserted that public opinion of neutrals had no effect in the last war. Contrary to that, when the final verdict of history is given it will be found that the losers lost not by lack of valor or courage. They lost not by lack of efficiency or even from starvation. They lost by failure to heed the public opinion of what were originally neutral nations. . . .

"Incidentally on Armistice Day in 1929 I made the part of this proposal relating to the immunity of food ships. It was approved by the leaders in a score of nations. Those nations who did not regard it with favor thought it one-sided. But they now find themselves hideously menaced from the air. The double proposal should now commend itself to those who then thought it one-sided. . . .

"To those who doubt the practicability of the idea of ships moving through blockades, I may point out that the Belgian Relief Commission delivered more than 2,000 full cargoes of food through two rings of blockade. It was done by international agreement under neutral management operating continuously for more than four years. It proved that this could be done.

"Moreover, the conventions as to the Red Cross were fairly well held to in the civilized countries during 1914 to 1919. The agreements as to protection of prisoners were also fairly well held. At least some agreements to mitigate barbarity have been kept in war. These growths away from barbarism lend hope for further progress toward protection to women and children.

"If we wish to lower our vision from the transcendent questions of humanity involved, we can find an impelling interest to neutrals in these proposals.

"In the last war the blockade initially reduced demand and every farmer in the world suffered. Then as the long lanes of food from the Southern Hemisphere could not be used because of diminished shipping and the submarine, the demand was concentrated on North America. And the farmers of the Southern Hemisphere went bankrupt during the war.

"Perhaps some one thinks our farmer benefited. He did not. He has for years and is today still suffering from the expansion of submarginal lands and the inflation of land values due to the high prices of the war. . . ."

VII

FOREIGN TRADE AND TRADE IN ARMS

ONE OF the greatest subjects of misrepresentation of Herbert Hoover is that concerning his policies upon international economic relations and especially upon the tariff. He is not, and never has been, an isolationist or a narrow-minded nationalist. His belief has been that of Alexander Hamilton who argued that the main objective of a·government should be a commercial policy that "was capable in intelligent hands of benefiting the nation as a whole." Also, that "an advantage to one man does not necessarily mean, when it is fairly examined, a corresponding burden imposed upon another."[1] In other words, Hoover believes that the United States should have a balanced economy, and that this can be reached by the export of raw materials and manufactures peculiarly adapted to production in this country, in return for the products likewise adapted to the economy of other nations. Tariffs, therefore, should aim primarily at the protection of the national economy as a whole and incidentally at the protection of specific interests. This is in direct contrast to the Congressional theory of protection which is that a tariff should be laid specifically to protect a certain industry and only incidentally to protect the national economy or general welfare of

[1]F. S. Oliver, *Alexander Hamilton*, p. 241.

124

all the people at large. In fact, this latter theory, as recently epitomized by Professor Frank Whitson Fetter of Haverford College[2] holds that "domestic producers are entitled to a 'preferential' position in the American market; because of lower costs abroad—principally labor costs—a tariff is necessary to insure this; competition between American producers prevents tariffs from raising prices; the test to apply in determining the need for higher rates is the increase in imports; tariffs help rather than injure our foreign trade; every one enjoys the benefit of the tariff; our position as a creditor nation is not to be given any consideration in the determination of our tariff policy."

But Hoover holds that, as far as possible, tariff rates should be determined in the light of the standard that would represent "the difference in the cost of production at home and abroad." No matter how difficult might be the attainment of this ideal, at least it is worth working for. Since changing times and circumstances must be taken into consideration, the only way to accomplish any approximation of this standard would be by means of the adjustment of specific rates at the hands of a bi-partisan Tariff Commission. This Commission should act by judicial process through open proceedings. This would substitute business principles for log-rolling and should get tariff-making out of the

[2]Article entitled, "Congressional Tariff Theory," published in the *American Economic Review*, September, 1933, p. 415.

political mire in which the Congressional theory, mentioned above, had always involved it during recent years.

Of course, Hoover's policy of a flexible tariff, rather than an embargo, aroused bitter opposition at the hands of Republican and Democratic tariff extremists and high protectionists, as well as the theoretical free-traders. Strange to say, they at once united and proceeded actively to oppose the above ideas of the Hoover Administration.

The Republican party platform of 1928 promised an increase in agricultural tariffs and a moderate revision of those on manufacturing industries. Furthermore, largely due to the importunities of Republican Senator William E. Borah of Idaho, Hoover had promised during the course of the campaign to call Congress into special session to pass needed legislation for farm relief and a moderate revision of the tariff. But when Congress met on April 15, 1929, pursuant to his call, it at once began a tariff revision which proceeded to disregard Hoover's expressed wishes and undertook a general revision which contained, according to the estimate of one of the Committee of Ways and Means of the House of Representatives, about 21,000 separate items.

While the bill received rather prompt consideration and passage by the Lower House on May 28, 1929, the Senate went through a long process of contest and delay which extended for more than a year so that the Smoot-Hawley bill, as it finally emerged, did not pass both Houses until June 16, 1930. It contained all the inconsistencies and abuses that might be expected from the prevalent system of log-rolling. And it is a matter of public record that altogether the Democratic senators cast more than 1,000 individual votes to maintain or increase specific tariff rates which they later declared to be excessive.[3]

During this time of legislative wrecking of his tariff policies, Hoover steadily fought to maintain his principles. At one time, by the combined action of the Republican high tariff Old Guard, the so-called Progressives, and the Democrats in the Senate, the flexible tariff provisions were defeated in the Senate. While the bill was in conference after it had been passed by both Houses, Hoover demanded that the flexible provisions be incorporated again in accordance with his views. This was accomplished. Hoover was only willing to accept the bill provided it contained the necessary provisions for its continued amendment by means of the flexible provisions at the hand of a bi-partisan Tariff Commission. Under these conditions he signed the bill and, under his direction, the Tariff Commission promptly began its work of revision.

While the Smoot-Hawley tariff was bitterly denounced by Franklin D. Roosevelt and the Democratic party in the campaign of 1932, the consistency of their position, or rather the lack of it, is amply shown by the fact that

[3]See *New York Times,* April 3, 1930.

it still stands upon the statute books eight years later and only slightly modified by Secretary Hull's Reciprocal Trade Agreements. All this seems to go far towards justifying the stand taken and the fight made by Herbert Hoover and his Administration. Furthermore there is the Democratic argument about the reasons for the debt repudiation by the Allies as due to inability to sell enough goods and make enough money transfers to the United States with which to meet the debt payments. This overlooks the clinching statement later made by Hoover which must be the final answer to all of this old thesis.

It is now a publicly established and acknowledged fact that, since the Allied governments ceased the payment of their installments on the debts, either their governments or their citizens have accumulated balances in the United States in gold or in the purchase of American securities of a minimum of four or five billions. That is their reserve today (1940) for purchase of war materials in the United States. That amounts, in other words, to perhaps twice the amount of the installments that are overdue on their debts. If they were able to transfer money to the United States for purposes of investment and reserves, it is the answer once and for all to the contention that they were prevented from payment by American trade policies.

During the Coolidge Administration an international treaty for the "Supervision of the International Trade in Arms and Ammunition and in Implements of War" had been signed at Geneva on June 17, 1925, by representatives of the United States and numerous other nations. This had not yet been ratified by the United States Senate so in a special message to Congress on December 10, 1931, Hoover urged that the Senate undertake the final consideration of the treaty.[4] He remarked, that "with the added impetus which ratification by the United States would lend to such a move, it is quite possible that the fourteen ratifications necessary by treaty stipulation would be received to bring the convention into force."

In June, 1932, President Hoover laid before the World Disarmament Conference, which was then sitting, among other recommendations a proposal that the weapons which could be used and are used to attack civil populations should be abolished. This recommendation included bombing planes, their ammunition, also poison gas and submarines. This proposal was approved by forty-one nations and declined by eight others.

Since the United States Senate continued to disregard his recommendations of 1931, Hoover returned to the subject as late as January 10, 1933. Although he had just been defeated for re-election, he again took up the cudgels and endorsed a policy which he thought would contribute to the peace of the world. Under this date he sent a message to Congress[5] in which he called

[4]*State Papers,* Vol. II, p. 81. [5]*State Papers,* Vol. II, pp. 565–566.

the attention of that body to the fact that recent events had but emphasized the urgent need for more authority in the Executive for the control of the shipment of arms from the United States for military purposes. The control of such shipments to areas of prospective and actual international conflict, he thought, would greatly aid the earnest efforts which all nations were making to prevent and lessen the dangers of such conflicts. It would be futile for one nation alone to engage in such prohibitions while other nations continued to supply arms. Also, this would tend to give an advantage to one nation over another by adding to the war preparations in manufactures and in increasing the skill of those nations which would not co-operate. He again earnestly urged that the treaty of 1925 should be ratified.

On the other hand if, as seemed probable at the time, it should prove impossible to secure ratification of this treaty by the Senate, he suggested, as an alternate policy, that legislation should be promptly enacted which should confer upon the President the authority to limit or forbid in his discretion the shipment of arms for military purposes in those cases where special undertaking of co-operation could be secured from other leading nations in the manufacture of arms. This would enable the Executive to place the United States in line, in special cases, with those other nations who might be willing to make like sacrifices for the purpose of preventing military conflict. Due to the attitude of non-co-operation on the part of President-elect Roosevelt and the Democratic leaders in both Houses of Congress, nothing was accomplished.

NOTE

To show the consistency of Herbert Hoover in his desire for preventing or ameliorating the horrors of war, attention should be called to the fact that during the time of the Congressional debates upon the subject of repealing the Neutrality Act during the autumn of 1939, soon after the beginning of the second European War, he issued a statement on October 10 which carried further the proposals of his former policy. He urged that the sale of defense weapons only be permitted and that legislation be passed which would prohibit the sale of bombing planes, bombs, poison gas and submarines for attacks on civilian populations or used for terrorizing purposes. This was in line with his above-mentioned proposal to the World Disarmament Conference in June, 1932.

In elaborating his proposals he stated as follows:

"I do not like to think of the day when bombing planes, engaged in the killing of women and children, on both or either side in this war, will be identified as the product of American manufacturers. Whichever country it may be, the news will be transmitted to the American people that this killing has been done with the products of American industry.

131

"Equally important, and from exactly the same reasoning, I am convinced that we should permit nations to buy from us the instruments by which they can defend themselves from such barbarities. We should therefore permit the sale of pursuit planes, light observation planes, anti-aircraft guns, and any other instruments of defense against attacks on civilians. . . .

"We would not be building up an excessive munitions industry, with its profiting from war and with its inevitable collapse in dislocation and increased unemployment. We would not be building up out of weapons themselves a consequential manufacturing or finance interest in our country, which could be an added nucleus for agitation that we go deeper and deeper into the war.

"The proposal largely meets the distrust that the repeal of the embargo is but another step in the program of joining the United States in this war. We would not be throwing the weight of our arms manufacture into European power politics; we would be throwing it toward greater humanity in the world and less destructive war. We would not be showing partiality to either side. . . .

"It is consonant with long declared national policies of the United States in respect to this sort of arms. It is not based on action for or against neutrals, who may be at war, as it would apply at all times against neutrals as well as combatants, before and after war occurs.

"By such action America would be again raising a

standard against barbaric action. By prohibiting the sale of these weapons of attack on civilians and permitting the sale of these weapons of defense of civilians we are not stepping deeper into this war but stepping away from pitfalls that may lead into it.

"The proposal keeps both our conscience and our neutrality right. With its foundations in morals and humanity, it is surer ground for America than foundations in international politics."[6]

Ten days later, on the evening of October 20, Hoover again returned to the subject and broadcast over the radio an "Address to the American People," in which he reiterated with great force and earnestness his advocacy of the above measures.[7]

[6]Statement in full may be found under date of October 11, 1939, in both the *New York Times* and the *New York Herald Tribune*.

[7]See *New York Times* and *New York Herald Tribune* for October 21, 1939.

VIII

THE REDUCTION IN LAND FORCES

As PREVIOUSLY stated, Hoover had seen the horrors of war at first hand. His experiences during the World War, and the years immediately succeeding it, had caused him not only to be a man of peace but also had filled him with a conviction of the necessity for taking long-term measures to reduce as far as possible the barbarism and consequent human suffering that must result whenever wars might be waged.

While Secretary of Commerce in the Cabinet of President Harding, he was moved to write to the latter a letter under date of May 11, 1921, in which he stated that since the Germans had accepted the indemnity, and thus the first step toward economic stability had been made, perhaps the time had arrived when a second great step might be taken. This step was disarmament. He added that "Our entrance into the Supreme Council makes such negotiations possible without calling international conferences or conventions. There is nothing that would give such hope of recovery in life and living as to have this terrible burden and menace taken from the minds and backs of men." Also he gave it as his mature judgment that "as Secretary of Commerce, if I were to review in order of importance those things of

134

the world that would best restore commerce, I would inevitably arrive at the removal of this, the first and primary obstruction to reconstruction and recuperation."

President Harding replied three days later, on May 14. He said that he hoped he need not assure Secretary Hoover that a step in the direction indicated would be "taken very earnestly" at the earliest day upon which the European situation might make it seem advisable. It is evident that Harding agreed with Hoover as to objective but not with regard to method. He was unwilling to undertake separate negotiations with Germany as Hoover suggested but must have had in mind at this date some such action as the calling of the Washington Conference for the Limitation of Armament which met on November the 12th following. As is well known this Conference was mainly occupied with the limitation of naval armaments as was likewise the Geneva Conference of 1927. The problem of the reduction of land forces and armaments remained practically unsolved. When Hoover became President he first turned his attention to a continuation of naval limitation and achieved the success of the London Conference of 1930 but still continued to keep in mind the extension of disarmament to other fields and forces.

He again followed a custom usual with him and took advantage of the opportunity afforded by a public address which he was to give before an organization, or

on some important occasion, to forecast or propose new
and weighty action. The occasion he now used was that
of a meeting of the International Chamber of Commerce
in Washington, D. C., where he delivered the opening
address on May 4, 1931. In this he stated[1] that considerable progress had been made in the limitation and
reduction of naval arms and the foundations had been
laid for further progress in the future. Also, that these
agreements had contributed greatly toward the reduction of the burden of taxes and toward the establishment of confidence and good-will among the signatory
nations. He went on further to say that within a short
time the principle nations of the world would meet to
discuss the broad question of reduction in land armament. He gave it as his opinion that of all proposals
for the economic rehabilitation of the world there was
none which compared in necessity or importance with
such a conference. While the United States had a less
direct interest in the reduction of land armament than
any of the other large nations, since its forces already
had been demobilized and reduced more than all others,
yet there was for this country "a vast indirect interest
in greater assurance of peace, order and the increased
economic prosperity of other nations." He made a direct
application of his thought by adding that "it is within
the power of businessmen of the world to insist that this
problem shall be met with sincerity, courage, and con-

[1]Entire address in *State Papers*, Vol. I, pp. 558–560.

structive action. It is within the power of statesmen to give to the world a great assurance for the future and a great moral victory for humanity."

The approaching conference to which President Hoover referred was the World Disarmament Conference which was convened by the League of Nations at Geneva on February 2, 1932. As a part of the policy which he was developing of increased co-operation with the League of Nations for humanitarian and social purposes without involvement in the peculiar interests of this organization, Hoover prepared to participate in and support the movement for the reduction of land armaments. He frankly stated in a message to Congress[2] on December 10, 1931, that the United States had accepted the invitation to take part in this Conference. That with a view to establishing an "atmosphere of confidence" for the opening of the Conference, more than forty governments, including all the principal military and naval powers, had joined in the principle of a one-year armament truce. This truce was the outgrowth of a proposal made during September, 1931, by Signor Dino Grandi, the Foreign Minister of Italy. It was designed to prevent the expansion of armaments during the months preceding the Conference in the hope of removing the threat of an immediate and sudden revival of competition in arms before and during the time of the meeting of the Conference. Hugh Gibson, American

[2]*State Papers*, Vol. II, p. 75.

Ambassador to Belgium, was designated by Hoover to head the American delegation.

The Conference met at the appointed time and proceeded to waste several months in futile discussion and with almost an entire absence of any constructive work. During the first weeks it became evident that the grave instability of Germany was the real danger to world peace. The American delegation, led by Hugh S. Gibson, Ambassador to Belgium, had several informal discussions with Chancellor Bruening of Germany which indicated the possibility of agreements in revision of the Treaty of Versailles that would greatly strengthen the situation of the democratic German government. The British and Italian representatives agreed that the program was promising. Taking advantage of Secretary Stimson's presence in Geneva, and with the approval of the President, an informal discussion was arranged with Chancellor Bruening, Premier Tardieu, Italian Foreign Minister Grandi, and Prime Minister Ramsay Mac-Donald, by the Americans. The German proposals were extremely moderate and gave real hope of strengthening the Republic, and facilitating a possible agreement upon disarmament. All those present except Premier Tardieu were favorable to Bruening's proposals. The refusal of the French premier, however, even to discuss the proposal wrecked the project. It is the way of fate that within a few months the German Republic fell before Hitler and a real hope of peace in Europe disappeared.

138

Hoover watched every step with the closest attention and finally lost all patience and decided to take things into his own hands to the extent of making specific and vital proposals in order to crystallize the discussion and accomplish some results. He worked out in his own mind a set of proposals which were of an entirely new order. In his private papers there are copies of a series of proposals dictated by him to his stenographer, corrected or added to in his own writing, and finally completed in a memorandum which he read at a meeting of his Cabinet at the White House in Washington on the morning of May 24, 1932. The final proposals which are Hoover's own creation are so far-reaching and important that the memorandum is herewith given in its entirety just as he read it. It is as follows:

"MEMORANDUM

May 24, 1932

"In view of the confinued economic degeneration of the world and of the ineffectiveness of accomplishment at the disarmament Conference, it may be desirable to consider a change in American policies in relation to this conference. It has been the well considered policy of the United States not to take the leadership of the conference because the problems are so essentially European, but to endeavor as a friend of all parties to secure that the governments primarily concerned should accept their real responsibilities and confine American activities to encouragement. The divisions and dissensions amongst them, the inability to get together on any constructive program; the economic situation in the world has become so much more acute, the need of the American people and the world generally for some lift in spirit. If it could be properly formulated some bolder constructive suggestion might help pull the world from this morass.

"1. The world is spending $5,000,000,000 a year on armament, a large part of which is unnecessary for the maintenance of internal order. The balance is expended upon fears of invasion. I presume 2/3 of this sum would be totally unnecessary if the military forces of the world could be reduced to the minimum necessary for police forces. If such a thing could be brought about the governmental debt of the world could be discharged in 20 years from these savings alone.

"2. Although we have made every human effort to curtail naval forces, we must recognize that the continuing naval strength of the leading powers is solely a relative matter and that it does bear some relation to the land armament (a solely European problem).

"3. We have already suggested that statistically and for visualization purposes the police component of armies should be separated from the defense components. Standards have been set up by the disarmament conference which enables these calculations to be made in respect to each country using the standard set for

Germany in the Treaty of Versailles as a basis of the police component. We have denominated the 'defense component' as a matter of relativity.

"If we assume that any progress has been made through the Kellogg Pact and the League we can assume that the need for the defense component has diminished relatively among the governments possessing such components.

"4. We have suggested that the world by agreement is now armed only for defense and as the dangers to the world are offensive action, therefore all major offensive weapons should be abolished which will render smaller defense components necessary and increase the potency of defense. It would also increase the importance of the Pact and the League processes of peace.

"5. The question of naval relations to this problem has been raised. Our American Navy is about $1,000,-000,000 in capital expenditure below parity with necessary early replacements. If we could secure a reduction of naval arms we could save this entire expenditure and make large savings in operation of forces at present maintained. If we were willing to take this step it is possible the British would also be willing. With ourselves and the British willing it is possible the Japanese might also join. Any step of this sort would of course involve a requirement that France and Italy should take part and such steps might in turn relieve demands upon

France for large land forces and in turn relieve Italy for her forces in defense against France, etc.

"6. As a result of these promises I am suggesting consideration of some proposal as follows:

"1. Reduce by one-third the battleship strength of the world as now settled in the Washington and London naval treaties.

"2. Abolish all aircraft carriers.

"3. Reduce cruiser strength provided for the three signatories of the London Treaty by one-third and require that France and Italy undertake no further construction of this category.

"4. Reduce destroyer strength provided for the three signatories of the London Treaty by one-third and require that France and Italy make no increase in tonnage above present construction.

"5. Abolish all submarines.

"6. Abolish all military aviation except for scouting purposes.

"7. Abolish all mobile land guns of more than 6-inch calibre.

"8. Abolish all tanks.

"9. Abolish poison gas.

"10. Reduce defense component of all armies by one-third.

"If such a program were announced with sincerity today it might give new hope and a new life to the entire spirit of the world. For the Disarmament Conference to dissolve with a mere minor agreement will be a calamity. Civilization is seriously jeopardized by continuation of its present arms.

"I recognize that armament is both a cause and effect of political instability and that while there are many points of political friction that need cure, yet they cannot be cured by any political agreements that the world is prepared to accept. But one of the contributions to [a] cure is the dissolution of fear which haunts the world as a result of its massed armaments."

In a press statement of June 22, Hoover covered this in a more popular form which also becomes an important document in the history of disarmament:[3]

"The following is the substance of instructions which have been given by the President to the American Delegation for guidance in the discussions which are now occupying them.

"The time has come when we should cut through the brush and adopt some broad and definite method of reducing the overwhelming burden of armament which now lies upon the toilers of the world. This would be the most important world step that could be taken to expedite economic recovery. We must make headway against the mutual fear and friction arising out of war armament which kill human confidence throughout the

[3] *State Papers*, Vol. II, pp. 211-213.

world. We can still remain practical in maintaining an adequate self-defense among all nations, we can add to the assurance of peace and yet save the people of the world from ten to fifteen billions of wasted dollars during the next ten years.

"I propose that the following principles should be our guide:

"First: The Kellogg-Briand Pact, to which we are all signatories, can only mean that the nations of the world have agreed that they will use their arms solely for defense.

"Second: This reduction should be carried out not only by broad general cuts in armaments but by increasing the comparative power of defense through decrease in the power of attack.

"Third: The armaments of the world have grown up in general mutual relation to each other. And, speaking generally, such relativity should be preserved in making reductions.

"Fourth: The reductions must be real and positive. They must effect economic relief.

"Fifth: There are three problems to deal with—land forces, air forces, and naval forces. They are all interconnected. No part of the proposals which I make can be disassociated one from the other.

"Based on these principles, I propose that the arms of the world should be reduced by nearly one-third.

"*Land Forces:* In order to reduce the offensive character of all land forces as distinguished from their defensive character, I propose the adoption of the presentation already made at the Geneva Conference for the abolition of all tanks, all chemical warfare and all large mobile guns. This would not prevent the establishment or increase of fixed fortifications of any character for the defense of frontiers and sea-coasts. It would give an increased relative strength to such defenses as compared with the attack.

"I propose furthermore that there should be a reduction of one-third in strength of all land armies over and above the so-called police component.

"The land armaments of many nations are considered to have two functions. One is the maintenance of internal order in connection with the regular forces of the country. The strength required for this purpose has been called the 'police component.' The other function is defense against foreign attack. The additional strength required for this purpose has been called 'defense component.' While it is not suggested that these different components should be separated, it is necessary to consider this contention as to functions in proposing a practical plan of reduction in land forces. Under the Treaty of Versailles and the other peace treaties, the armies of Germany, Austria, Hungary and Bulgaria were reduced to a size deemed appropriate for the maintenance of internal order, Germany being assigned 100,000 troops for a population of approximately

65,000,000 people. I propose that we should accept for all nations a basic police component of soldiers proportionate to the average which was thus allowed Germany and these other States. This formula, with necessary corrections for powers having colonial possessions, should be sufficient to provide for the maintenance of internal order by the nations of the world. Having analyzed these two components in this fashion, I propose as stated above that there should be a reduction of one-third in the strength of all land armies over and above the police component.

·"*Air Forces:* All bombing planes to be abolished. This will do away with the military possessions of types of planes capable of attacks upon civil populations and should be coupled with the total prohibition of all bombardment from the air.

"*Naval Forces:* I propose that the treaty number and tonnage of battleships shall be reduced one-third; that the treaty tonnage of aircrift carriers, cruisers, and destroyers shall be reduced by one-third, and that no nation shall retain a submarine tonnage greater than 35,000.

"The relative strength of naval arms in battleships and aircraft carriers, as between the five leading naval powers, was fixed by the Treaty of Washington. The relative strength in cruisers, destroyers, and submarines was fixed, as between the United States, Great Britain and Japan, by the Treaty of London. For the purposes of this proposal, it is suggested that the French and

Italian strength in cruisers and destroyers be calculated as though they had joined in the Treaty of London, on a basis approximating the so-called accord of March 1, 1931. There are various technical considerations connected with these naval discussions which will be presented by the delgation.

"*General:* The effect of this plan would be to effect an enormous saving in cost of new construction and replacements of naval vessels. It would also save large amounts in the operating expenses in all nations of land, sea and air forces. It would greatly reduce offensive strength compared to defensive strength in all nations.

"These proposals are simple and direct. They call upon all nations to contribute something. The contribution here proposed will be relative and mutual. I know of nothing that would give more hope for humanity today than the acceptance of such a program with such minor changes as might be necessary. It is folly for the world to go on breaking its back over military expenditures and the United States is willing to take its share of responsibility by making definite proposals that will relieve the world."

It was a direct, honest, and effective means of carrying out the purpose for which the General Disarmament Conference had been convened. It could be applied with a minimum of negotiation with regard to the adjustment of details. It embodied two definite American policies. The first of them was to promote general disarmament, both from altruistic motives and in order to share in the resulting economic benefits. The second was to keep our own armament at least up to the minimum defensive requirements, both for economy and in conformity with our national traditions. Of course, action under the second policy was dependent upon the success of the first, since our then existing armament could not be further reduced without general disarmament.

The plan stated clearly its guiding principles. It reaffirmed the Briand-Kellogg Pact. It proposed to deal with the controversy over both quantitative and qualitative reduction, based on existing relative strength and applied to land, sea, and air forces as a whole; also to reduce both man power and mechanical offensive power. The principle of basing reduction on percentage above police components was sound and practical and might be extended if it proved to be initially successful and offered a solution to the demands for equality in armament made by the powers that had been defeated in the World War. On the other hand, the application of the principle was an element that required agreement by negotiation as to figures. Of course, Hoover realized that it threatened the ascendancy of the French army and he expected it to be resisted by the French Government—as it was. Nevertheless, he felt he was on the right track and went ahead.

The proposal to reduce the strength of mechanical offensive power was probably the most important part and is likely to have the most lasting effect on world thought with regard to armament. That proposal was to abolish bombing planes, submarines, mobile land guns of more than six-inch caliber, and tanks and poison gas.

The effect would have been greatly to increase the defensive strength of the smaller nations through fortifications and otherwise. Hoover's idea was that if these offensive mechanical weapons were abolished by all governments, then if they should ever go to war there would not be time to recreate them for an effective attack.

Some comment was made among writers on armament that this distinction between weapons was an impracticable one. But this was not the case, as the weapons designated for abolition were positive and specific. Furthermore, the practicability of this idea was supported by the American General Staff at the time, and further was supported by the Technical Committee of the Arms Conference on the same practicable grounds. Had it been adopted such attacks as that made by the Germans on the Poles in September, 1939, when the Polish army was destroyed by the offensive mechanical weapons, would have been impossible.

It is one of the notable things in the spread of ideas that discussion today on methods of disarmament still revolves around this proposal of Hoover's. President

Roosevelt, on May 18, 1933, again proposed these ideas to the heads of fifty-four nations, but without any reference to the action of his predecessor. Also in the discussions in 1936, Hitler again advanced this same general idea.

The proposal for further naval reduction was both concrete and practical. It used treaty strength, rather than actual strength, as a basis for reduction. This was to the advantage of the United States, since our country was further below already-existing treaty allowances than were other major powers. For this reason, Hoover anticipated the opposition of France and Japan to this proposal. We may surmise that its adoption would weaken the French position on land and the British position on the sea; therefore, all these powers might covertly, if not openly, oppose his plan. But Hoover was convinced that it was so simple and practical that it could be adopted if there existed a real desire for international agreement. In conclusion it may be stated that the proposals embraced the reduction of armies to one third over the number required to preserve internal order and the abolition of arms used for offensive purposes.

Hoover first instructed, through Secretary Stimson, Ambassador Gibson privately to sound out the members of the Conference with regard to these proposals. Some of the members expressed private approval but nothing resulted.

Prime Minister Ramsay MacDonald was among the British delegates at Geneva and his close friendship with Hoover was an added advantage in that the matter was discussed by the British and American representatives with extreme frankness. In the strictest confidence and for his personal information, Hoover caused the substance of his proposals and the plan of action to be divulged to MacDonald before these things were brought out in public. Hoover learned from private outside sources that MacDonald regarded the proposals with great favor. Also, he was informed that the British delegation seemed in full accord with regard to the restriction of land and air armaments. On the other hand, MacDonald was concerned about the attempt to modify the agreements made at the London Naval Conference in 1930. He felt that these agreements were so carefully adjusted and had been reached with such difficulty that far-reaching consequences might result from any change in them. He was especially apprehensive in case there should be further reduction in cruisers, in the light of the troubled situation in the Far East. While cruiser reduction was not ruled out, MacDonald felt an opportunity for further serious consideration would be absolutely necessary.

It was also known that MacDonald felt himself to be in a very awkward situation since, without his authority, a member of his delegation, Sir John Simon, had committed himself to join with the French in forming a united front. This was against his expressed wishes and without his knowledge. Furthermore, this same British delegate seemed reluctant to make a frank admission of his action to the members of the American delegation as MacDonald had desired him to do. All in all, MacDonald showed the most sincere desire to cooperate fairly and openly with Hoover in the attempt of the latter to advance the cause of world peace.

Hoover's next step was, in spite of protest from some of our delegation, to instruct Ambassador Gibson to make the plan public in order, if possible, to arouse a favorable world public opinion. This was done in the form of a note addressed to the Conference and drafted by Hoover himself. It was read to the Conference by Gibson and, as already quoted on a preceding page, made public by means of a press statement released by Hoover in Washington on June 22, 1932.

The Conference adjourned until the following year in order to consider these proposals further. The election of Franklin D. Roosevelt in November, 1932, brought to an end the American efforts to secure some results out of the Conference. As will be shown later on, Hoover proposed to use the debt of the United States as a measure of pressure for accomplishing these proposals, but his suggestion was rejected by Roosevelt.

IX

THE FAR EAST

WHEN Mr. Hoover assumed the office and duties of the Presidency in March, 1929, the Kellogg-Briand Peace Pact was in process of signature by various nations as already has been stated. The number of signatures had reached fifty-five by the close of the year. Among them were China and Russia, between whom, during the summer of this same year, a controversy leading to a dangerous situation had arisen in Manchuria. This resulted in conflict between Russian and Chinese armed forces.

It will be remembered that President Hoover and Prime Minister MacDonald had issued a joint statement, carried in the morning newspapers[1] of October 10, 1929, in which they said that both the British and American Governments were resolved to accept the Kellogg-Briand Peace Pact not only as a declaration of good intentions but also as a positive obligation to direct national policy in accordance with its pledge. In harmony with this statement, President Hoover and Secretary Stimson were of the opinion that if the Peace Pact were to amount to anything beyond an expression of pious intentions some action should be taken to bring

[1]*State Papers*, Vol. I, pp. 107–9.

the force of public opinion to bear upon the controversy between Russia and China. With the hearty support of the British Government, they approached the diplomatic representatives of various countries involved in the Nine Power Treaty of 1921, which guaranteed the independence of China, and which also were signatories of the Kellogg Pact. These countries, under the lead of the American Government, brought simultaneous pressure upon the Russian and Chinese Governments with the result that hostile forces were withdrawn, negotiations were carried through, and an agreement was signed between the two countries on December 22, 1929. By means of this successful action, both international strength and respectability were given to the Kellogg Pact.

Some two years later, in September, 1931, a newer and more direct danger to the peace of the world arose from the Japanese invasion of China. Under the leadership of the military forces in Japan the Government of that country invaded Manchuria with its armed forces. The Hoover Administration considered this a violation of the Nine-Power Treaty in which Japan had joined with the other powers, having special interests in the Far East, in an agreement to respect the integrity of China. It may be mentioned that the Kellogg Pact likewise was violated and it was clear also that this would lead to violation of the Open Door Policy as well.

Secretary of State Stimson in his valuable and inter-

esting book entitled, *The Far Eastern Crisis*,[2] states
that on October 9, 1931, he had discussed the matter in
all its aspects before the Cabinet. The following day he
had a long conference with the President, who evidently
had been thinking over the matter since Stimson's discussion of the day before and now "plunged vigorously
and sympathetically" into the problem. He expressed
himself as ready to enter into some action that might
parallel that anticipated from the Council of the League
of Nations, to which China had appealed, but without
involving ourselves in the activities of that international
organization of which we were not a member. Hitherto
Hoover had been engrossed with the problems arising
from the depression and the recent financial collapse in
Europe, but he now found it necessary to give deep
thought to the whole matter of the Far Eastern problems. Hoover had lived for some years in the Orient,
which gave him a keen insight into the whole matter.
Also, it was fortunate that Secretary Stimson had first-
hand acquaintance with the Far East and had recently
returned from the Philippines, where he had been Gov-
ernor-General.

[2]Published for the Council on Foreign Relations by Harper and
Brothers, New York, 1936, pp. 60–61. At the beginning of his Admin-
istration President Hoover offered the post of Ambassador to Japan
to the Honorable Roy O. West of Chicago, Illinois, who recently had
been Secretary of the Interior in the Cabinet of President Coolidge.
Mr. West felt compelled, by reasons of domestic character, to decline
the honor. This post of responsibility was successively occupied by
Honorable Charles MacVeagh of New Hampshire, Honorable William
R. Castle, Jr., of Washington, D. C., and Honorable W. Cameron
Forbes of Massachusetts.

It was about this time that Hoover read to a Cabinet meeting a memorandum in which he laid before the members his analysis and conclusion with regard to the Far Eastern problem to which, as he then said, he had given deep consideration. This memorandum in summary was as follows:[3]

"The whole transaction is immoral. The offense against the comity of nations and the affront to the United States is outrageous. But the Nine-Power Treaty and the Kellogg Pact are solely moral instruments based upon the hope that peace in the world can be held by the rectitude of nations and enforced solely by the moral reprobation of the world. We are not parties to the League of Nations, the covenant of which has also been violated.

"The problem lies in three parts:

"First, this is primarily a controversy between China and Japan. The United States has never set out to preserve peace among other nations by force and so far as this part is concerned we shall confine ourselves to friendly counsel. In this connection we must remember some essentials of Asiatic life. Time moves more slowly there; political movements are measured in decades or centuries not in days or in months; that while Japan has the military ascendancy today and no doubt could take over parts or all of China, yet the Chinese people possess transcendent cultural resistance; that the *mores*

[3]Summary printed in Wilbur and Hyde, pp. 600–601.

of the race have carried through a dozen foreign dynasties over three thousand years; that the Chinese are ten to one in population. No matter what Japan does, in time they will not Japanify China, and if they stay long enough they will be absorbed or expelled by the Chinese. For America to undertake this on behalf of China might expedite it but would not make it more inevitable.

"There is something on the side of Japan. Ours has been a long and deep-seated friendship with her and we should in friendship consider her side also. Suppose Japan had come out boldly and said:

" 'We can no longer endure these treaties and we must give notice that China has failed to establish the internal order these treaties contemplated. Half her area is Bolshevist and co-operating with Russia, the government of Manchuria is in the hands of a military adventurer who ignores the Chinese Government, and China makes no effort to assert her will. That territory is in a state of anarchy that is intolerable. The whole living of our people depends upon expanding the sales of our manufactures in China and securing of raw materials from her. We are today almost economically prostrate because there is no order in China. Beyond this with Bolshevist Russia to the north and a possible Bolshevist China on our flank, our independence is in jeopardy. Either the signatories of the Nine-Power Pact must join with us to restore order in China or we must do it as an act of self-preservation. If you do not join we consider we cannot hold to an obligation around which the whole environment has changed.'

"America certainly would not join in such a proposal and we could not raise much objection.

"Second, our whole policy in connection with controversies is to exhaust the processes of peaceful negotiation. But in contemplating these we must make up our minds whether we consider war as the ultimate if these efforts fail. Neither our obligations to China, nor our own interest, nor our dignity require us to go to war over these questions.

"These acts do not imperil the freedom of the American people, the economic or moral future of our people. I do not propose ever to sacrifice American life for anything short of this. If that were not enough reason, to go to war means a long struggle at a time when civilization is already weak enough. To win such a war is not solely a naval operation. We must arm and train Chinese. We would find ourselves involved in China in a fashion that would excite the suspicions of the whole world.

"Third, we have a moral obligation to use every influence short of war to have the treaties upheld or terminated by mutual agreement. We should co-operate with the rest of the world; we should do so as long as that co-operation remains in the field of moral pressures. As the League of Nations has already taken up the subject, we should co-operate with them in every field of negotiation or conciliation. But that is the limit. We will not go along on war or any of the sanctions either economic or military, for those are the roads to war."

Shortly after this, in a message on Foreign Affairs, sent to Congress[4] on December 10, 1931, Hoover made public statement of his policy. He called attention to the fact that this country had been deeply concerned over the situation in Manchuria. As a party to the Kellogg-Briand Pact and to the Nine-Power Treaty we had a responsibility in maintaining the integrity of China and a direct interest with other nations in maintaining peace there. When the controversy between China and Japan originated in September the League of Nations was in session and China appealed to the Council of that body, which at once undertook measures of conciliation between the two countries. Hoover stated that it seemed both wise and appropriate to aid and advise with the League, and thus have unity of world effort to maintain peace, rather than to take independent action. But in all negotiations the Department of State had maintained complete freedom of judgment and action as to participation in any measures which the League might finally determine upon.

He continued: "Immediately after the outbreak of the trouble this government advised both Japan and

[4]*State Papers,* Vol. II, pp. 76-77.

China of its serious interest. Subsequently it communicated its views to both governments regarding their obligations under the Kellogg-Briand Pact. In this action we were joined by other nations signatory of the pact. This government has consistently and repeatedly by diplomatic representations indicated its unremitting solicitude that these treaty obligations be respected. In the recurring efforts of the nations to bring about a peaceful settlement this government has realized that the exercise of the utmost patience was desirable, and it is believed that public opinion in this country has appreciated the wisdom of this restraint."

It is important that here should be stressed the fact that the United States had no legal standing in the League of Nations, hence it could take no definite part in the activities of that organization. It could only confer and co-operate by means of sympathetic and parallel action. It was careful to preserve the attitude of impartiality between China and Japan but at the same time it insisted that treaty obligations should be respected.

The next move is vividly described by Secretary Stimson.[5] The Department of State had decided upon the note of January 7, 1932, in which both China and Japan were informed that the United States could not admit the legality of any situation, nor did it intend to recognize any treaty or agreement entered into between

[5]*Far Eastern Crisis*, pp. 95–97.

those governments or agents thereof, which might impair the treaty rights of the United States or of its citizens in China. Furthermore, the statement was made that the United States Government did not intend to recognize any situation, treaty, or agreement, which might be brought about by means contrary to the covenants and obligations of the Kellogg-Briand Pact. But the story of Hoover's part in it should be told in Stimson's own words.

"The only differences of opinion that I remember [concerning the note] were as to its scope and the definiteness and finality of its method of expression. But I felt that it was a serious decision and one on which the President should be consulted. On the evening of January 4, I therefore laid the matter before him at the White House. He was awaiting me in his study in the room which had been Lincoln's Cabinet office. It was at a time of great economic stress. The procession of countries which had followed Great Britain off the gold standard was putting serious pressure upon our own resources. World currencies were fluctuating and depreciating. . . . The drain on our gold and the withdrawal of foreign deposits were putting a strain on our domestic banks, thereby stifling our industry. Unemployment was rapidly rising.

"Furthermore, the new Congress under changed party leadership was not co-operating with the recommendations for the purpose of meeting this crisis which the President had made to it when it met in December. On the very day of my visit he had sent them a further urgent message hoping to expedite their action and to awaken public support for the long series of constructive remedies which he had previously urged upon them. The burden thus weighing upon him showed itself clearly in his face. It seemed almost fantastic to expect him to be able to turn from this domestic pressure, under which he was the pivot upon which turned the work of reorganizing our entire domestic economy, in order to consider new complicated problems arising out of a crisis in the Orient."

These various negotiations not only failed to check the aggression of the Japanese in Manchuria but also, during the last of January, the Japanese attacked Shanghai. Hoover at once ordered a strong contingent to that city, both of American troops and of naval forces. The entire Asiatic Squadron was collected at Shanghai under the command of Rear Admiral Montgomery Taylor. Reinforcements also were sent to the American bases in the Hawaiian and Philippine Islands and strict orders were issued that our forces should confine themselves to the task of protecting Americans. Meanwhile, certain nations that were members of the League of Nations demanded that economic sanctions should be imposed upon Japan. This idea seemed to have the support of the State Department and was especially appealing to the judgment and ideas of Secretary Stimson, who continually advocated this policy. Hoover not only strongly opposed this policy but placed his personal veto upon it on the ground that such a policy would lead directly to war. In place of it he developed with Stimson's assistance the plan that all nations should agree that they would not recognize the acquisition of territory which might be obtained in violation of the Kellogg-Briand Pact. This policy was agreed upon by the principal nations, but the situation in the Far East, so far as China and Japan were concerned, remained in *status quo* to the end of the Hoover Administration.

As his term of office was drawing to a close, Hoover formed the opinion that the verbal discussions during these negotiations should be properly recorded. For this reason he requested Secretaries Ray Lyman Wilbur and Arthur M. Hyde, members of his Cabinet, to prepare memoranda of these to be added to his other files.

The two following letters are worthy of full quotation since they show that President Hoover himself originated the policy of non-recognition of territorial settlements which resulted from aggressive action in violation of the terms of the Kellogg-Briand Pact. The first is from the Secretary of War, Patrick J. Hurley, and is as follows.

"WAR DEPARTMENT
"WASHINGTON

January 19, 1933

"My dear Mr. President:

"I have read your letter of the thirteenth instant.

"I do recall the discussion in Cabinet meetings on the subject of the Japanese invasion of Manchuria.

"The first discussions on that subject in which I participated were in the beginning of November, 1931, shortly after my return from the Orient. During the month of December, 1931, you outlined on several occasions to the Cabinet your doctrine of non-recognition. In connection with that doctrine, you discussed fully the obligations of the United States and of Japan toward China under the Kellogg-Briand Pact.

"I had never heard of the non-recognition doctrine in relation to the Kellogg Pact until it was announced by you in the Cabinet.

"At the time we were all aware of the resolution of the Inter-American Congress of 1890, which declared that 'the principle of conquest shall not during the continuance of this treaty of arbitration be recognized as a principle under American public law.' We also were aware that on May 11, 1915, the then Secretary of State (Mr. Bryan) said: '. . . The Government of the United States has the honor to notify the Imperial Japanese Government that it cannot recognize any agreement or undertaking which has been entered into or which may be entered into between the Governments of Japan and China, impairing the treaty rights of the United States and its citizens in China, the political or territorial integrity of the Republic of China, or the international policy relative to China commonly known as the Open Door Policy. . . .'

"Notwithstanding the history of the principle of non-recognition, you were the first to make application of that doctrine as an instrument of the Kellogg-Briand Pact. You announced to the Cabinet in December, 1931, the Non-Recognition Doctrine as an instrument of the Kellogg-Briand Pact as the policy of your Administration on the subject of the Japanese invasion of Manchuria.

"I was present when you requested the Secretary of State to prepare for your consideration a statement of the doctrine. I was not present when the reading of the first public announcement of the doctrine was agreed upon. I presume that that occurred between you and the Secretary of State, as I do not recall the subject of the exact wording of the doctrine being discussed in Cabinet.

"Respectfully yours,
(Signed) "Patrick J. Hurley."

"The President
"The White House."

The other letter is from Ray Lyman Wilbur, the Secretary of the Interior.

"THE SECRETARY OF THE INTERIOR
"WASHINGTON
"January 26, 1933

"My dear Mr. President:

"Your request of January 13, that I make note of my recollections of the development of the non-recognition policy in connection with the aggressive action of Japan in Manchuria, is of unusual interest to me.

"As Chairman of the Institute of Pacific Relations for two sessions in 1926 and 1928, I became acutely conscious of the dangers in the Manchurian situation and of Manchuria as the tinder box of Asia. In the Cabinet, I followed the development of the policy of this country in this matter with the keenest interest. As you know, I have been in Manchuria and Northern China and Japan. This added a personal interest to the happenings in Mukden and the later extensions of Japanese authority over Manchuria.

"From the very first, the discussions in the Cabinet took on a serious turn. The breach of the Nine-Power Treaty and the Kellogg Pact presented at once the problem of some form of individual action by us or united action on the part of a number of nations. Some members of the Cabinet felt that only by strong means and united action on the part of the nations involved could the Japanese be restrained. The State Department was firm in this attitude and presented its program of seeking united action by the nations involved.

"From the very first discussions, you, as President, with your Oriental experience, visualized the inevitable future steps that would follow upon any decision once made in this field. Your insistence upon the policy of non-recognition of whatever territorial conquests the Japanese might make was presented so vigorously and efficiently that it soon dominated over all other ideas. Its wisdom was brought out by future developments. At the time of the Shanghai incident, with the menace of involvement every hour, the temptation for more aggressive action had to be reconsidered, but your advocacy of the policy of non-interference, of avoiding conflict in every reasonable way, consonant with the protection of American life, and of not recognizing any territorial gains or other advantages from breaches of the existing treaties, gradually crystallized into a definite policy. Negotiations with other nations and with the League of Nations soon placed your non-recognition doctrine on a national and international basis.

"I recollect that upon one particular occasion, after a discussion of the dangers and difficulties involved, and the pressure from the State Department for united aggressive action, confusion was created in the minds of all. But you then made a clearcut statement based upon your long experience in China of just what the Oriental psychology was, of the danger of interference at the present time, of the evident impotence of the League, of the unwisdom of any military action, and of the advantage of non-recognition, not only as a basis for action in this particular difficulty, but in other breaches of treaties. Out of these discussions and decisions and the public discussions accompanying them came the Hoover doctrine.

"Very sincerely yours,
(Signed) "Ray Lyman Wilbur."
"The President,
"The White House."

As already stated, the policy of the imposition of economic sanctions had been considered for some time by the State Department, since it appealed especially to Secretary of State Stimson. A short time before the expiration of his term of office, President Hoover went on record as finally and absolutely opposing any such policy, in a memorandum to Secretary Stimson in writing, under date of February 23, 1933: "As you are aware, I have all along been inflexibly opposed to the imposition of any kind of sanctions except purely public opinion. The imposition of any kind of sanction, military or economic, would, in the present state of mind of the Japanese people, provoke the spread of the conflagration already in progress and might involve the United States.

"As it is not our intention to ever engage in sanctions other than that of public opinion, it would seem to me that some occasion should be taken to make it clear.

It would certainly relax the tension to some extent. It would in no way undermine the importance of public opinion in this controversy for under the non-recognition doctrine that would be continuous and will ultimately be triumphant.

"The whole doctrine of non-recognition is not alone a method of invoking world opinion but it is equally important in the phase that it avoids precipitant action and allows time to work out proper solutions. It occurs to me therefore that we should make it clear somehow. It would, I believe, relax a considerable amount of present tension.

"Yours faithfully,
Herbert Hoover."

Another matter which was supposed to have been settled during the latter part of Hoover's Administration, but in a way contrary to his wishes, was that of the independence of the Philippine Islands. It is still a subject of vexation, both to the Roosevelt Administration and the American people, although nearly ten years have passed since that time.

According to Hoover's view, the Philippine Islands should be given their independence provided there was a complete and absolute separation. This must relieve the United States from all responsibility for the defense of the Islands. Also, he insisted that the economic stability of the Islands, after their separation from the customs union with the United States, should be assured. He was opposed to any conditional separation which would place upon us responsibility without authority. He was of the opinion that the economic stability of the Islands was not yet attained, so, in order to settle his doubts he caused Secretary of War Hurley to proceed to the Islands to examine the situation and report upon the results.[6] Upon Secretary Hurley's return Hoover issued a Press Statement[7] on October 27, 1931. The President said that the Philippine question had been the subject of lengthy discussion at a Cabinet meeting that same day but with no final policies as yet formulated and that such discussions would be continued in the future. He called attention to the fact that independence had been promised to the people of the Philippines directly or indirectly by every President, since their annexation, and by Congress. However, the problem was one of time. The time element involved the necessity that independence must be assured of durability with a stable government. Hoover was convinced that immediate independence without assured economic stability would result in collapse of governmental revenues and of all economic life in the Islands.

In spite of Hoover's opposition, the Democratic Congress passed a bill during December, 1932, granting independence to the Philippine Islands. Hoover returned the bill to Congress with a veto message[8] on

[6]Wilbur and Hyde, p. 610.   [7]*State Papers,* Vol. II, p. 24.
[8]*State Papers,* Vol. II, pp. 569–76.

January 13, 1933. In this able State Paper he asserted: "Our responsibility to the American people is that we shall see the fact of Philippine separation accomplished without endangering ourselves in military action hereafter to maintain internal order or to protect the Philippines from encroachment by others, and above all that this shall be accomplished so as to avoid the very grave dangers of future controversies and seeds of war with other nations. We have a responsibility to the world that having undertaken to develop and perfect freedom for these people we shall not by our course project more chaos into a world already sorely beset by instability. The present bill fails to fulfill these responsibilities. It invites all these dangers. It does not fulfill the idealism with which this task in human liberation was undertaken. . . .

"During the period of intermediate government prior to complete independence, not alone the internal and external political relations of the Philippine people must be adjusted, but they must adjust their economic life to the complete abrogation of the present free-trade association with the United States. The period for such adjustment in this act is too short, too violent. . . .

"A large part of the motivation for the passage of this bill is presumed relief to certain American agricultural industries from competition by Philippine products. We are trustees for these people and we must not let our selfish interest dominate that trust.

"The bill weakens our civil authority during the period of intermediate government to a point of practical impotence. . . .

"During this period, however, the American flag will be flying and our army will be in occupation.

"The income of the Philippine Government has never in the past been sufficient to meet, in addition to other expenditures, the cost of supporting even the Filipino Scouts, much less an army or navy. . . .

"We are dealing with one of the most precious rights of men—national independence interpreted as separate nationality. It is the national independence of 13,000,-000 human beings. We have here a specific duty. The ideals under which we undertook this responsibility, our own national instincts and our institutions which we have implanted on these islands, breathe with these desires. It is a goal not to be reached by yielding to selfish interests, to resentments, or to abstractions, but with full recognition of our responsibilities and all their implications and all the forces which would destroy the boon we seek to confer and the dangers to our own freedom from entanglements which our actions may bring. Neither our successors nor history will discharge us of responsibility for actions which diminish the liberty we seek to confer nor for dangers which we create for ourselves as a consequence of our acts. This legislation puts both our people and the Philippine people not on the road to liberty and safety, which we desire, but on the path leading to new and enlarged dangers to liberty and freedom itself."

The Philippine Independence Act was promptly passed over Hoover's veto, but succeeding events have established the soundness of his views. The people of the Philippines are themselves becoming aware of this. There would seem to be no subsequent reason for him to revise his judgment or to doubt the soundness of the position he took.

X

THE VISIT OF PREMIER LAVAL
WAR DEBTS AND FOREIGN LOANS

It was during the spring and summer of 1931 that a second and more serious depression came upon the countries of Central Europe, the consequences of which were immediately felt in the United States. It is well established today that the causes of this economic and financial collapse may be attributed in large part to France and its mistaken policies. The sequence of events was as follows. On March 21, 1931, was announced the agreement upon a customs union between Germany and Austria. On March 25 Great Britain demanded that this action be reviewed by the League of Nations. This was followed by the announcement of the French Government that it would not permit the agreement to go into effect. Evidently in order to serve as a threat against any such further plans, France also took further action, the results of which reverberated throughout the world. That country was a large holder of German and Austrian short-term securities, amounting to upwards of $200,000,000. The French demanded payment and this started a drain upon the finances of Germany and Austria. Although this was intended as a political measure, the financial results were disastrous. These two countries began to borrow or attempt to borrow elsewhere and a veritable panic spread over Central Europe.

The situation went from bad to worse and its reverberations were felt in the United States where the depression, which had shown signs of improvement under the leadership of President Hoover, took a decided turn for the worse. The situation in Europe finally became so critical that on June 19 a direct appeal for help was made to President Hoover by President von Hindenburg of Germany. Hoover now took matters in his own hands. By working night and day and by conference over the telephone with thirty out-of-town Congressional leaders he formulated the plans for and carried through the celebrated Moratorium. According to this and at the suggestion of this country the definite proposal was made for the postponement during one year of all payments on all inter-governmental debts, reparations and relief debts, both principal and interest. This of course did not include obligations of government held by private parties. Subject to confirmation by Congress, which action was assured by the approval of most of the Congressional leaders who were consulted, the American Government offered to postpone all payments upon the debts of foreign governments to it which were payable during the fiscal year beginning July 1, 1931. This was conditioned on a like postponement for one

175

FOREIGN POLICIES OF HERBERT HOOVER

year of all payments on inter-governmental debts which were owing to the important creditor powers.

The offer was tentatively accepted by all the powers addressed with the exception of France, which showed some sign of hesitation and demanded special terms. Hoover refused to listen to these. Immediately after the proposal the whole world breathed easier. Prices rose, employment increased, hope was revived, panics ceased. But with the French delay hope gradually receded, prices gave way, panic conditions again began to appear. When the French finally accepted under pressure of a strong statement from Hoover, it was already too late.

Hoover now was faced with a new emergency that threatened to bring down certain American banks and portended a financial panic in the United States.

But the national and international financial situation immediately had so improved that Secretary of State Stimson, believing that the matter was in process of definite settlement, left on June 25 for a holiday in Europe. Within a few days the situation had again turned for the worse as above stated and it appeared that Central Europe was in peril of a complete collapse. Hoover was compelled to act and he proceeded to take strong measures. He was supported by Acting Secretary of State William R. Castle who, in the absence of Secretary Stimson, became Hoover's main reliance in the subsequent negotiations. There was full co-operation on the part of Castle and he bore the main responsibility, ably assisted by the Acting Secretary of the Treasury, Ogden Mills. Secretary of the Treasury Mellon likewise was in Europe.

The acute phases of the trouble centered upon the inability of certain Central and South American governments, and their private institutions, to meet short-term obligations. These trade bills, bank acceptances and short-term loans had been piled up by Germany and Central European countries on the one hand, and by South American countries on the other, to an unprecedented amount. They had been sold all over the world in order to stave off taxes, to support the unemployed and for social and economic purposes. They were bought mainly by British, Scandinavian, Dutch, Swiss and American banks, under the name of "trade bills" (*i.e.*, drafts accompanying shipment of goods), which many of them were not. The French were not greatly involved, as they had cashed their bills. The default on the bills, probably to a total of four billion dollars, threatened to ruin large American banks as well as British and other like institutions. It meant world-wide panic and destruction.

The French solution was that the United States lend sufficient sums to Germany to tide that country over the crisis. Hoover absolutely refused to entertain any such idea. He did not propose that the United States should be used as a cat's-paw by the French. He demanded that an immediate meeting of the creditor nations be held in London. On July 17 he cabled to Secretary Stimson and Secretary of the Treasury Mellon, who were both in Paris, a definite plan for them to present at the forthcoming conference of the creditor powers which was to open in a few days in London (July 20). This plan subsequently became the "Standstill" agreement, by which all the banks in the nine or ten nations that held the major part of the German short-term bills agreed not to present them for payment for a stipulated time. The plan was adopted by the London Conference on July 23.[1]

As may be imagined, the hesitant and selfish policy followed by France in this crisis created an unpleasant impression in America. The French Government soon became aware of this and also was rather jealous of the visit, two years before, of Prime Minister MacDonald of Great Britain which had resulted in such friendly relations between the British and American Governments. Premier Laval let it be known, through diplomatic means, that he desired an invitation officially to visit the United States. President Hoover, although he did not know definitely what Laval wanted until after the latter's arrival, formally invited him on September 24, 1931, to visit Washington to discuss the world economic situation. Laval further let it be known that he intended to place his cards upon the table and have a

[1] For more detailed account see Myers and Newton, *Hoover Administration*, pp. 81–106.

full and frank discussion of all matters of concern to both countries. It was understood that no matters at variance between the two Governments should be barred from the discussion. It may be mentioned here that the British Government was fully informed of the intended visit and was much pleased by the prospect of closer friendship and increased co-operation between the French and American powers.

As may be imagined, Hoover at once got into touch with the leading governmental and financial authorities in this country and, as usual, was thoroughly and well informed upon all matters that might become the subject of conversation in the personal interviews between himself and Premier Laval. He realized that in various ways the discussion of financial and economic questions would connect with the discussion of political questions. On the other hand, since the subjects under discussion would be very technical and Premier Laval's visit would be a short one lasting for only a few days, only broad general principles could be explored and the details of any subject would have to be deferred for future negotiations.

Laval arrived in New York on Thursday, October 22, 1931. Just before sailing from France he announced the personnel of his party. He brought with him seven of the most important financial authorities of France.

Laval was met at the Battery in New York City by Secretary Stimson and other officials, including a Committee appointed by Mayor James J. Walker. He was conducted to the City Hall where he was formally received by the Mayor. The crowds were large and unusually enthusiastic. The party then proceeded to the Pennsylvania Railroad Station and departed on a special train for Washington. Upon their arrival in that city Laval went to the home of Ambassador Walter E. Edge, our Ambassador to France, which was placed at his disposal during his stay in Washington. At six o'clock that same afternoon Premier Laval and his daughter arrived at the White House to be formally presented to President and Mrs. Hoover. At eight o'clock in the evening there was a State Dinner in honor of Premier Laval and also of Marshal Petain who was in Washington at this time. The dinner was a large one, some eighty people being present, and a number of representatives of official and journalistic Washington were there to meet the guests. After dinner was concluded some time was spent in informal conversation. Very pleasant relations were at once established between the President and the Premier.

The first formal conference between them did not take place until the next afternoon (Friday, October 23) at 3:30 o'clock. There were present President Hoover, Secretary Stimson, and Ogden Mills, the Acting Secretary of the Treasury. And on the French side, Premier Laval, and M. Jacques Bizot. The conference lasted until 6:45 P.M. when it adjourned until 8 o'clock.

The same five dined at the White House and continued the discussions until midnight. Ogden Mills interpreted what Laval said and Bizot interpreted what Hoover said.

After both sides had discussed in review the difficulties and dangers in the world, it was suggested there were three subjects that might be examined. The first was disarmament, to lift the political dangers and the economic pressures upon the whole world. The second was a readjustment of German reparations, if necessary, to extend the Moratorium and thus give the democracy a chance of survival. The third, the maintenance of the gold standard in the world.

On the subject of disarmament, Laval held that little could be done unless it was accompanied by guarantees of security to France or some sort of consultative pact that would lead in that direction. Hoover said that the American people could not and would not guarantee the security of any country; that they would not become involved in any agreement that might lead to military consequences in Europe; that the real security of France must rest upon the progress of peace in the world, and that this could be greatly advanced by a reduction of armaments all around.

On the question of German reparations Laval contended that there were no dangers to German democracy, but that the Germans themselves were dangerous and obstinate. He presented the idea that no concession to Germany could be made without a similar concession in the war debt of France to the United States. He further suggested there should be an international conference called for review of the whole question of inter-governmental debts. Hoover stated that the debts to the United States were individual agreements with each country; that they were not subject to international action; that they had been settled by individual agreement upon the basis of the capacity of each individual country to pay; that the United States had greatly reduced the French debt and settled it not upon the basis of German reparations but upon the ability of France to pay; that this ability to pay had been agreed by both sides to be correctly estimated at the time of the settlement; and that if the ability of France to pay had changed, the question must be taken up with the Congress of the United States and authority secured to revise the estimate of this ability. Both Laval and Hoover were aware that at that time France held some $600,000,000 of deposits in American banks. This amount was sufficient to pay installments on the debt for several years. Laval did not press the point further. Both did agree that at least an inquiry should be made into the situation in Germany as to whether or not estimates of her capacity to pay after the Moratorium needed revision for the period of the depression.

Over forty nations had at that time abandoned gold as a basis of currency, and the maintenance of the gold standard was in jeopardy throughout the world. Hoover and Laval agreed that France and the United States must maintain the gold standard if there was to be any hope of ultimate currency stability in the world, and that assurances should be given to the world that the two nations would remain constant in this policy. It also was agreed that it was too early to move toward a world monetary conference.

The conferences between the French and American officials continued throughout the following two days, Saturday and Sunday, October 24 and 25. M. Laval and his daughter spent the night of the 24th as the guests of Secretary and Mrs. Stimson at "Woodley," their country home in the suburbs of Washington. Among the guests invited to meet them at dinner were Senator William E. Borah, of Idaho, and Senator David A. Reed, of Pennsylvania. Senator Borah, in spite of his ability and political experience, had just made a very vigorous and undiplomatic statement with regard to American relations to Europe which had caused quite a sensation in both the American and European press. Secretary Stimson, by bringing Borah and Laval together and by the use of great tact, was able to smooth over a somewhat embarrassing situation. Laval left Washington in good humor at midnight on Sunday the 25th and sailed for Europe from New York at midnight on Monday, October 26.

As a result of long discussion in which President

Hoover, Secretaries Stimson and Mills, also Premier Laval, M. Bizot, and Ambassador Claudel took part, a joint statement was prepared and issued on October 25 which stated [2] in large part as follows: "The traditional friendship between the United States and France, the absence of all controversy between our two governments, a record of many events in collaboration toward peace of the world, embracing among its recent phases the adoption of the Kellogg-Briand Pact, render it possible and opportune for the representatives of our governments . . . to explore every aspect of the many problems in which we are mutually interested. . . . Relations of mutual confidence between governments have the most important bearing upon speeding the recovery which we seek. We have engaged upon that mission with entire frankness. We have made real progress.

"We canvassed the economic situation in the world, the trends in international relations bearing upon it; the problems of the forthcoming conference for limitation and reduction of armaments; the effect of the depression on payments under inter-governmental debts; the stabilization of international exchanges and other financial and economic subjects.

"An informal and cordial discussion has served to outline with greater precision the nature of the problems. It has not been the purpose of either of us to

[2]Printed in full in *State Papers*, Vol. II, pp. 19–21.

engage in commitments binding our governments, but rather, through development of fact, to enable each country to act more effectively in its own field.

"It is our joint purpose that the conference for limitation of armaments will not fail to take advantage of the great opportunity which presents itself and that it will be capable of meeting what is in reality its true mission, that is the organization on a firm foundation of permanent peace. In so far as inter-governmental obligations are concerned we recognize that prior to the expiration of the Hoover year of postponement, some agreement regarding them may be necessary covering the period of business depression, as to the terms and conditions of which the two governments make all reservations. The initiative in this matter should be taken at an early date by the European powers principally concerned within the framework of the agreements existing prior to July 1, 1931.

"Our especial emphasis has been upon the more important means through which the efforts of our governments could be exerted toward restoration of economic stability and confidence. Particularly we are convinced of the importance of monetary stability as an essential factor in the restoration of normal economic life in the world in which the maintenance of the gold standard in France and the United States will serve as a major influence.

"It is our intent to continue to study methods for

the maintenance of stability of international exchange.

"While in the short time at our disposal it has not been possible to formulate definite programs, we find that we view the nature of these financial and economic problems in the same light and that this understanding on our part should serve to pave the way for helpful action by our respective governments."

It should be mentioned here that the Germans, on November 19, 1931, acted under the terms of the reparations agreements, and the Lausanne Conference followed in May, 1932. President Hoover proposed to Congress in December, 1931, a temporary readjustment of the debt payments to those countries which needed it during the depression but Congress refused any concession. The ultimate effect of this attitude and of further actions during the following year was the practical repudiation of the war debts by the debtor nations and the consequent loss of any payments, with a resulting loss to the American taxpayers.

Of course, during the time of the visit of Premier Laval the Democratic smearing machine was in full action. Certain Democratic newspapers claimed that there was a concealed intention on the part of President Hoover to cancel the war debts. The President denied this publicly on October 9, 1931.[3] He added, with regard to the extension of the Moratorium, that: "It is not customary among decent individuals or amongst nations

[3]Myers and Newton, p. 135.

to insist upon a debtor making payment beyond the capacity of the individual or nation to pay, but that does not imply that they shall not pay to the full extent of their capacity. In fact, it is one of the foundations of moral and economic life."

On the morning of November 18, 1931, a story appeared in one of the newspapers to the effect that the United States had sent a note to France in order to clarify the Hoover-Laval conversations. At his press conference, held the same day, Secretary Stimson made the following explicit statement:[4]

"There has been no change whatsoever in the attitude of the United States towards the procedure under discussion in Europe in regard to the European problem of reparations as originally expressed in the Hoover-Laval communiqué. No change in this attitude is in contemplation. No new proposal whatsoever has been made by the United States in regard to the inter-governmental debts due it nor has the subject even been discussed. The cables exchanged between the State Department and its Embassies have been only for the purpose of keeping us informed regarding the situation in Europe, and we are not in any way participating in the European negotiations."

Even after the lapse of eight years the story of a secret agreement between Hoover and Laval with regard to war debts has been revived. In his interesting book

[4]U. S. Department of State, Press Releases, Weekly Issue No. 112, p. 419.

187

entitled, *After Seven Years*,[5] Raymond Moley makes the statement in describing the events leading up to the conference between President-elect Franklin D. Roosevelt and Moley on the one side and President Hoover on the other in Washington, D. C., on November 22, 1932:

"Finally—and this was the core of our doubts and misgivings—we wondered if there was any truth in the rumor that the President had promised Laval or MacDonald, when these gentlemen visited him, that he would attempt to bring about a complete readjustment of the debt situation. Men close to Laval openly made this claim. Considering the customary mendacity of French diplomats about matters affecting French vital interests, we weren't disposed to place much credence in it. Still, it was significant that the British seemed to believe it. (I was later flatly told by three of the highest British officials that such had been the import of President Hoover's conversations.) At any rate, this unknown factor loomed so large in our reckonings that on one of the cards Roosevelt himself scribbled—not for the purpose of asking the direct question, presumably, but to remind him of the situation during the conference—the notation 'secret agreements by Pres.' "

It may be emphatically stated that these suspicions and innuendoes are entirely without foundation. To the extent that the discussions between Hoover and Laval

[5]Published, 1939, Harper and Brothers, New York, pp. 71–72.

dealt with the subject of debts and reparations, they were entirely limited to steps of a temporary character which might be taken to offset the effects of the depression. President Hoover took his stand upon the definite American position that the payment of the war debts to the United States was not in any way contingent upon the payment of German reparations but was based solely on the capacity of each individual debtor to pay as the latter might be affected by the depression. No cancellation or revision of either debts or reparations was proposed by either side. No assurances or commitments on such a subject were either asked for or given. The communiqué given out, on October 25, 1931, at the close of the discussions, was an accurate statement in all these respects.

It is appropriate to introduce at this point a discussion of the real attitude of President Hoover with regard to foreign loans by American citizens. The subject of flotation of foreign loans by the banks in the United States has been under a great deal of discussion and misrepresentation. As a matter of fact, such loans were not of much importance during the Hoover Administration for, after the depression had begun in 1929, the making of loans to foreign countries was practically at an end for the whole period of his administration. However, his attitude in these matters is of importance as a contribution to American foreign policies of government.

This attitude was clear long before Hoover came to the Presidency. In 1922, soon after he became Secretary of Commerce, a conference was called at the White House of the representatives of banks issuing foreign bonds. Hoover participated, and took an important part in this conference. The bankers agreed to submit all proposed loans to the State Department and a committee including Hoover was appointed to pass upon all issued. A notice to that effect was issued to the public on March 3, 1922. But the bankers soon became disturbed by this curb and a protest was sent by Governor Strong of the New York Federal Reserve Bank. This protest being submitted to Hoover, he prepared a memorandum on the subject for Secretary of State Hughes,[6] in which he insisted strongly that certain standards should be set in regard to these loans. The standards upon which he insisted were that all American capital sent abroad should be invested in reproductive works and not used for the balancing of budgets or military or other wasteful expenditure; that by reproductive use of these loans they would create wealth out of which they could be repaid; and that otherwise it was a destruction of capital and might result in great losses.

He also made several public statements upon this subject, notably in May, 1922, in October, 1923, and again to the Pan American Commercial Conference in 1927 in which he insisted vigorously that foreign loans

[6]Wilbur and Hyde, *The Hoover Policies*, p. 35.

should be subjected to inspection and to publicly established standards. The Harding and Coolidge Administrations, however, refused to undertake the responsibility for rigid conditions in this connection.

While the subject was of little practical importance during Hoover's Administration, and little business of this sort was undertaken, nevertheless in a message to the Pan American Commercial Conference of October 8, 1931, he stated that:

". . . such loans . . . are helpful in world development provided always one essential principle dominated the character of these transactions. That is, that no nation as a government should borrow or no government lend and nations should discourage their citizens from borrowing or lending unless this money is to be devoted to productive enterprise.

"Out of the wealth and the higher standards of living created from enterprise itself must come to the borrowing country the ability to repay the capital. Any other course of action creates obligations impossible of repayment except by a direct subtraction from the standards of living of the borrowing country and the impoverishment of its people.

"In fact, if this principle could be adopted between the nations of the world—that is, if nations would do away with the lending of money for the balancing of budgets for purposes of military equipment or war purposes, or even that type of public works which does not bring some direct or indirect productive return—a great number of blessings would follow to the entire world."[7]

Early in the year 1932 efforts were being made to resume such foreign loans, so Hoover addressed the following letter to the Secretary of Commerce, R. P. Lamont.

"January 9, 1932

"The Honorable
The Secretary of Commerce
Washington, D. C.
"My dear Mr. Secretary:

"As you are aware the Department of Commerce for many years has been solicitous in respect to the character of foreign loans being issued in the United States. No authority has existed by which any more than purely factual interest in them could be taken except the willingness of bankers to accept views of the State Department as to their effect upon foreign relations of the government. You will recollect the various speeches I made on the subject of the necessity of reproductive character of foreign loans offered to the American public particularly the address to the Investment Bankers Association and to the Pan American Commercial Conference which are typical. There is in the Department a good deal of information on the whole subject.

"I have never been able to bring myself to believe

[7]*State Papers*, Vol. II, pp. 7–8.

in government regulation to determine the business risks of such offerings as it leads into very definite moral obligation by the government to the subscriber if there be failure of security, and it brings great possibilities of international friction. On the other hand economically a domestic loan may be inadequately secured but it does not represent a parting with national wealth such as may be implied in the purchase of foreign securities which fail. These loans therefore become a matter of more than normal public interest.

"But some way the American people have a right to know more accurately the business risks of foreign loans offered to them. It has occurred to me that it would be worth investigating one method of control in connection with issues of such foreign loans. In a number of countries vendors of securities to the public by way of public issues are required to publish prospectuses containing certain essential facts as to the profits of vendors, the intrinsic situation of the borrowers, the purposes for which the money is to be used, etc., and any misstatements or inadequacy of statement renders the vendors liable to the subscribers.

"I would be glad if the Department would investigate, through your legal division, the foreign laws on the subject; also if you would give some thought to the character of information which should be required in such prospectuses in order to give essential protection to the investor. That is such requirements as profits of the vendor, the financial condition of the borrower, the purposes for which the money is borrowed, etc.

"As to the purposes for which monies are borrowed, it might be well to consider a series of categories which might be required to be expressed, for instance if the money is borrowed for purposes of support of military equipment or action; if it is borrowed for the purpose of balancing budgets; if it is borrowed for refunding of previous loans which themselves represent either of these objects; if it is borrowed for reproductive purposes and as to the estimated earnings which would be the result of the loan, whether it be indirectly in public works or directly in private enterprise. Other ideas will no doubt occur to you.

"Yours faithfully,
(Signed) "Herbert Hoover"

Secretary Lamont replied to this letter as follows:

"DEPARTMENT OF COMMERCE
Office of the Secretary
Washington, D. C.
January 15, 1932.

"The Honorable
The President of the United States
White House
Washington, D. C.
"My dear Mr. President:
"In response to your letter of January 9, 1932, re-

garding the desirability of measures for safeguarding foreign loan flotations in this country, I transmit two memoranda. One is on the subject, 'Foreign Laws Governing the Sale of Securities;' the other on 'Foreign Government Control of the Issuance of Foreign Bonds and the Requirements of the New York Stock Exchange for Listing Foreign Bonds.'

"The first memorandum contains summaries of the provisions of law in Great Britain, France, and Germany, regulating the issuance of these securities and does not cover the flotation of foreign government obligations.

"The second memorandum discusses briefly the methods of control actually exercised by foreign governments in the matter of the issuance of foreign government obligations in their markets. These data show that such control, in the cases of Great Britain, France and Germany, is of an informal or extra-legal character. They also show that the New York Stock Exchange has sought to safeguard the issuance of foreign securities in this market by requiring the submittal of a considerable amount of data regarding each foreign loan before the same is listed on the Exchange.

"To put into effect the safeguards mentioned in the last two paragraphs of your letter, three courses of action might be pursued, namely (1) enactment of Federal legislation, (2) a restatement of the foreign loan policy of the State Department, and (3) the incorporation of these safeguards in the listing requirements of the New York Stock Exchange.

"(1) *Federal Legislation.* The Commercial Laws Division raises the question whether a law regulating the sale of securities, domestic or foreign, would be constitutional. Decisions of the Supreme Court in certain insurance cases suggest that the Court might hold that the sale of securities is not commerce and that any law regulating such sale does not come within the scope of the commerce clause of the Constitution.

"(2) *Restatement of Foreign Loan Policy.* While this would be desirable, the question arises whether it would be effective in preventing the issuance of unsound securities, especially since the right of the Government to pass on proposed foreign issues has been questioned. There is the further question as to the obligation which the Government might assume in passing upon the soundness of foreign issues.

"(3) *Action by the New York Stock Exchange.* If the New York Stock Exchange could be induced to incorporate the suggested provisions in its requirements for listing, the results desired would be attained to a fairly satisfactory degree. This would be an application of the general principle that business should, in the public interest, seek to regulate its own affairs as far as possible.

"Since there is doubt as to the practicability of the first two of these proposed measures, I am inclined to favor the third. I should judge that, under present conditions, the New York Stock Exchange would be disposed to give serious consideration to such a proposal and to act favorably thereon.

"Sincerely yours,
(Signed) "R. P. Lamont"

In the course of the Presidential campaign, during the following summer of 1932, Governor Roosevelt of New York revived the unfair and untrue charge continually harped upon by the smearing machine of the Democratic party organization that the Hoover Administration had connived at the sale of foreign securities to unsuspecting Americans. In answer to this, the Department of State issued the following press release in categorical denial of these charges. It is herewith reprinted in order that the matter may be settled once and for all.[8]

"August 21, 1932
"FOR THE PRESS
"*Statement by the Department of State:*
"In his speech on Saturday Mr. Roosevelt said that if he were elected he promised 'that it will no longer be possible for international bankers or others to sell to the investing public of America securities on the im-

[8]Department of State, Press Releases, Weekly Issue, No. 152, pp. 127–8.

197

plied understanding that these securities have been passed on or approved by the State Department or any other agency of the Federal Government.'

"This is an insinuation that the Department has thus assisted the bankers in the past. It would be interesting to know whether Mr. Roosevelt intends to revive this long since discredited story and whether he will assert that the Department has actually thus assisted the bankers.

"The facts have repeatedly been stated. The Department of State has never approved a single foreign loan. It advised the bankers not to make loans to countries which had not funded their debts to the United States, thereby speeding up the negotiations which resulted in the debt agreements.

"At one time the Department warned bankers planning to advance loans to Germany of the dangerous over-extension of credit to that country and of the probable difficulties of collection due to the provisions of the Treaty of Versailles. It undoubtedly through its advice thus prevented many loans. On the other hand it has never encouraged the issuance of any loans whatsoever. Any assertion to the contrary is untrue and is so understood by the people of the United States."

Another slander upon Hoover is that his Administration actively encouraged the investment by the American people of untold billions of dollars in Europe prior to the financial collapse of 1929 and that the subsequent

losses were due to the speculation and unsound investments consequent thereupon. A study of "The International Financial Position of the United States" made
in the year 1929 by Ralph A. Young, prepared for and
printed by the National Industrial Conference Board
Inc. of New York City, would seem to prove conclu-
sively that,[9] "Taken as a whole . . . America's recent
investment capital exports were partly offset by investment capital imports and the remaining balance was
more than offset by the net inward movement of interest,
dividend and capital repayment funds, especially in the
last seven years. Contrary to opinion, the nation as an
economic unit has not been placing larger and larger
amounts of its available liquid capital supplies abroad,
but has been mainly accumulating foreign securities by
reinvesting interest, dividends and capital repayment
sums received each year. The varying character of
short-term capital payments and credits was a final
factor contributing to an 'adverse' balance of international capital payments in some years and a 'favorable' balance in other years."

Charges of his personal responsibility for losses on
foreign loans, again being made in the campaign of
1936, Hoover replied in an address on October 17 of
that year at Philadelphia, as follows:

". . . President Roosevelt made the statement that
between 1920 and 1930 eight billions of money out of

[9]Page 269, published Philadelphia, 1929.

American pockets had been sent to foreign countries and used by them to give employment to their citizens. He says that most of that money is gone for good. He implies that it was taken away from American workmen and given to foreign workmen. That reflects mostly upon my predecessors in office, including President Wilson. But I shall not let that smear rest upon them. President Roosevelt did not mention that this money was borrowed by foreigners on interest and was not gifts. He does not mention that it was borrowed from private Americans and not from our Government.

"I have had each of these foreign borrowings which were offered to the American public carefully traced. I am informed their total was seven billions, not eight billions. That is, however, an error of only 12½ per cent and we can let that pass. Of these seven billions that are supposed to be lost, two billions have become due and have been paid in full. Three billions are not yet due but interest and amortization are being met regularly. The remaining two billions are partly in default but are being recovered as the world recovers. The net result is that this is an error of about 87½ per cent.

"But even that is not the whole story. It is an economic fact that loans to foreigners must ultimately be transmitted in goods, services or gold. Gold was probably not shipped. Therefore these private loans made employment of American workmen and American farmers in producing this amount of goods. In fact those private loans contributed greatly to full employment in the United States during the whole decade of the twenties when unemployment existed in practically every country in the world. President Roosevelt's statement is the more astonishing as he has himself advocated the loaning of money to foreigners, including Russia, thus to create markets for products of American shops and farms. He created the so-called Export Banks for this exact purpose. But in his case he has placed the risk on the taxpayer and not upon the private banker."

XI

DISCUSSIONS WITH PRESIDENT-ELECT ROOSEVELT

I. WAR DEBTS, STABILIZATION OF CURRENCIES, AND A WORLD ECONOMIC CONFERENCE

THE FINANCIAL collapse in Central Europe which began in Austria in April, 1931, has already been mentioned. It was followed by a series of panics and the abandonment of the gold standard by about forty countries. This led to financial, trade, and general economic chaos. As shown in the preceding chapter, President Hoover and Premier Laval, at the time of Laval's visit to Washington in October, 1931, had discussed the subject of the world stabilization of currencies, and a world economic conference. As a result of their discussions, it was decided that the time had not yet arrived when a world conference might be called.

Hoover, some seven months later, on May 24, 1932, authorized Secretary of State Stimson to open conversations with Prime Minister MacDonald of Great Britain upon the subject of summoning an international monetary and economic conference. On the following day, May 25, Secretary Stimson, by means of the transatlantic telephone, talked with Prime Minister MacDonald and presented to him the President's views.

These were as follows: The time now was favorable for calling an economic conference which should be separate in its agenda from the question of German reparations. At a time of increasing economic difficulty it was urgent that the world be encouraged by some constructive action. Since the British were off the gold standard, it would seem desirable that they should call the conference, for the United States had a stable currency and no import quotas. Hoover further desired that the conference should not be merely a meeting of experts but that Prime Minister MacDonald should personally head the conference which, if possible, should consist of the ablest men of each nation.

MacDonald gave his approval and the American Ambassador to Great Britain, Andrew W. Mellon, was now instructed to place these views formally before the British Government. The President worked continually upon the problem of calling the conference and even had determined upon the men whom he would send as American delegates. He felt that it would be necessary for the delegates to get to work in preparation for the conference as soon as possible after the approaching November election. Otherwise, the conference might be indefinitely postponed and international discouragement and economic depression be increased.

In the meantime each of the nations which were to be represented in the coming conference chose a body of experts which met at Geneva on November 1, 1932.

The American representatives were: Ambassador Frederick M. Sackett, our Ambassador at Berlin, Mr. Norman H. Davis, Professor Edmund E. Day, and Professor John H. Williams. A program for the conference was formulated and in addition the representatives at this preliminary meeting showed unanimity in a report upon the urgent necessity for prompt agreement to end destructive international competition and also took the first steps in the preparation of methods to accomplish its purpose.[1]

Another complication arose about this time from the fact that the Moratorium would expire shortly after the November 8 election which was to decide upon the political complexion of the next Administration. Hoover realized that several of the governments involved would need, in all probability, a temporary extension of the Moratorium. He was confident that this need did not apply to France, which country had made large gold deposits in the United States. Hoover also was firmly persuaded that the whole matter, as repeatedly stated, was one for discussion between the United States and each country individually, the determination of the question to be based upon the capacity of each country to pay. If any long-term concessions were to be made, this should be only in return for specific advantages to the American people.

[1] A detailed account of this whole subject, with the succeeding conferences with President-elect Roosevelt, may be found in Myers and Newton, Chapter XV, and Wilbur and Hyde, pp. 506–523.

A new and disturbing element was introduced on November 10, 1932, two days after the Presidential election, in which the Hoover Administration was decisively defeated and it became known that a new Democratic Administration, under the leadership of Franklin D. Roosevelt, would take office on March 4, 1933. All of the debtor governments, in words that were almost identical, requested a suspension of all payments pending a complete review of the entire debt question prior to the December 15 payments which would soon be due. These governments obviously were acting in concert in order to take advantage of any change in policy or counsels in our national leadership in expectation of the inauguration of a new President. This was followed by a flood of propaganda in this country which was designed, in great part, to discredit the Hoover Administration. It was of the greatest importance that this action on the part of our debtors should be firmly and frankly met with a united front by the people of the United States.

President Hoover had returned to his home in Palo Alto, California, in order to cast his vote but immediately conferred with the State Department in Washington by telephone. On his return trip to the East, which followed immediately, he wired to President-elect Roosevelt from the train at Yuma, Arizona, under date of November 12, 1932. In this telegram he summarized the situation, gave his own views, and pointed to the

fact that any negotiations which might now be begun
would necessarily extend beyond the remaining period
of his own Administration. He suggested that he and
Mr. Roosevelt confer personally at some convenient
date as the policy of the United States must be settled
to a great degree before December 15. Hoover was informed that Roosevelt was contemplating a trip to the
South, so he suggested that the latter might stop in
Washington some time during the ensuing week for
the purposes of this conference. The President also
stated his willingness to have Mr. Roosevelt bring to
the conference any Democratic leaders or advisers as he
might wish.

Roosevelt did not reply for two days but explained
the delay by the fact that he was suffering from a slight
cold. The *New York Times* let it be known that this cold
did not prevent Roosevelt from conferring with Louis
McHenry Howe, Colonel Edward M. House, and Ber-
nard M. Baruch. His reply to Hoover, which was received by the latter when his train reached Hutchinson,
Kansas, was as follows:

"WESTERN UNION TELEGRAM
"1932 November 14—7:23 A.M.

"THE PRESIDENT
"Hutchinson Kansas

"I appreciate your cordial telegram. On the subjects
to which you refer, as in all matters relating to the

welfare of the country, I am glad to co-operate in every appropriate way, subject, of course, to the requirements of my present duties as Governor of this State.

"I shall be delighted to confer with you in Washington, but I have been confined to the house with a slight cold and I am, therefore, not able to suggest a definite date. I shall call you on the telephone as soon as the time of my departure for the South has been determined.

"May I take the liberty of suggesting that we make this meeting wholly informal and personal. You and I can go over the entire situation.

"I had already arranged to meet a number of the Democratic leaders of the present Congress late this month at Warm Springs. It will be helpful for me to have your views and all pertinent information when I meet with them. I hope that you also will see them at the earliest opportunity because, in the last analysis, the immediate question raised by the British, French and other notes creates a responsibility which rests upon those now vested with executive and legislative authority.

"My kindest regards.

(Signed) "FRANKLIN D. ROOSEVELT."

After Hoover's arrival in Washington on Thursday, November 17, he telephoned Roosevelt inviting him to the White House and suggesting that he bring a technical adviser as he wished some one representing Roosevelt to meet with the technical men in the Administration.

Hoover's message continued: "I had expected to call on either Tuesday [22d] or Wednesday [23d] a meeting of the ranking members of the two finance committees as I have to make a reply to these foreign countries. I was wondering whether you would like to have me call them an hour after you have come into conference with me and we could go on and have a time with them about it.

FDR "Yes, I was planning to stop over at the Mayflower on Tuesday night and see them Wednesday morning before I go to Warm Springs."

HH "There is one thing in the whole thing that requires immediate action and that is the reply to those countries."

FDR "Yes, that is right."

HH "There are other things that need ironing out with respect to their commitments, but the one definite thing is a note of reply that we should send to them."

FDR "That is right. Perhaps we could do that on Wednesday morning."

HH "Get the leaders in on Wednesday morning together."

FDR "Fine. I will see you on Tuesday then. Thank you."

The following telegram, now among Mr. Hoover's private papers, evidently was sent after the above conversation over the telephone. It refers to the fact that President Hoover had called a conference of Congressional leaders for the morning following their meeting. He also had proposed to the President-elect that if the two of them should agree on a policy, they should jointly meet the Congressional leaders. It would seem that frankness and co-operation could go no further.

"Albany, N. Y., Nov. 17, 1932
"THE PRESIDENT
"Washington, D. C.

"Thank you for your telegram. In pursuance of my thought expressed to you in my first telegram that our conversation should be wholly personal and informal, it seems best that I should determine whether it is proper for me to attend your conference on Wednesday with Senate and House leaders at White House after you and I have talked on Tuesday afternoon. Professor Raymond Moley will come with me on Tuesday.

(Signed) "FRANKLIN D. ROOSEVELT."

Raymond Moley, in his book entitled *After Seven Years,* gives an extended description of the conference between Hoover and Roosevelt which took place on

209

November 22,[2] at which he and Ogden Mills, Secretary of the Treasury, were also present. He makes the significant statement (page 68) that he and Roosevelt had "concluded that the President could scarcely have chosen a field in which there was less probability of sympathetic co-operation between the two administrations." This statement shows that partisanship and domestic politics were to be most influential in the coming future foreign policy and perhaps explains the vacillations and inconsistencies in this field during the time of the Roosevelt Administrations.

Says Moley (page 73): "Hoover plunged into a long recital on the debt question. He spoke without interruption for nearly an hour. Shyness, at the beginning, seemed to make him fix his eyes on the beautiful seal of the United States woven into the red carpet. After a while he began looking at me as he talked—a circumstance about which I had no more reason to be pleased than the inanimate carpet. He obviously found it hard to overcome the profound personal disappointment of the election, for he glanced at Roosevelt only occasionally, and then turned his eyes away again.

"Before he had finished, it was clear that we were in the presence of the best-informed individual in the country on the question of the debts. His story showed a mastery of detail and a clarity of arrangement that compelled admiration."

[2]Pp. 68–76.

Hoover's frank statements were met with vacillation and evasion. He proposed that a delegation should be selected at once in order that they might have ample time to prepare for their task. He also proposed that they should simultaneously deal with the war debt question, with the stabilization conference, and should co-ordinate with the World Disarmament Conference then in session. In Hoover's judgment all these problems must be interrelated if we were to secure real results. Furthermore, he offered full co-operation with Roosevelt in the naming of the delegates, and in the subsequent negotiations. According to Moley (page 75): "When Hoover reached the end of his recital, F. D. R. nodded his head in partial agreement." However, Roosevelt rejected the idea of any delegation and suggested that Hoover negotiate through our ambassadors and ministers. It may be remarked that this was impractical since action must then be taken in many capitals and, furthermore, no agreement would be binding upon Roosevelt. Also, no nation would be likely to negotiate merely with an administration which would expire in less than four months.

As already stated, Hoover had called a conference of Congressional leaders for the following morning. He therefore proposed to the President-elect that if the two of them agreed on a policy, they should jointly meet the Congressional leaders. Governor Roosevelt appeared to agree with the program, but he felt that he would rather not attend the White House meeting with Congressional leaders; that he himself would see the Democratic members at once.

It was decided that the President should issue a memorandum of principles and methods in accord with their discussion and the President-elect also should issue a statement. It was agreed that the President should prepare his memorandum for issue the following day, and that Secretary of the Treasury Mills and Professor Moley should meet finally to settle the two memoranda.

On the morning of November 23, the President met with the Congressional leaders of both parties and reviewed the entire war-debt situation with them and the necessity for national solidarity. The Democratic members, however, opposed the whole program and stated that they would not co-operate with it. When Secretary Mills called upon Mr. Roosevelt to settle the promised statements, it was suggested that President Hoover should issue his own memorandum and that the President-elect would comment upon it afterward. The President's statement of November 23 thereupon was issued to the press. It went fully into the whole question, for a better public understanding of the problem.[3]

President-elect Roosevelt issued his separate statement the same day.[4] The main substance may be found in the following paragraphs:

[3]State Papers, Vol. II, pp. 487–493.
[4]Printed in Myers and Newton, pp. 287–288.

"As to the debt payments due December 15, I find no justification for modifying my statement to the President on November 14 when I pointed out that 'the immediate questions raised by the British, French and other notes create a responsibility which rests upon those now vested with executive and legislative authority'.

"With regard to general policies respecting these debts I firmly believe in the principle that an individual debtor should at all times have access to the creditor; that he should have opportunity to lay facts and representations before the creditor and that the creditor always should give courteous, sympathetic and thoughtful consideration to such facts and representations."

War debt payments were made on December 15 by the most important debtors with the exception of France. The Government of that country openly claimed there was an assurance from President-elect Roosevelt that payment was not absolutely necessary for negotiations. This was due to an unfortunate press dispatch from Warm Springs, Georgia, where the President-elect was resting. It purported to express the view of Roosevelt that he did not regard payment of the December 15 installment to be a necessary condition for the opening of negotiations for debt adjustment. Mr. Roosevelt denied that the statement had any authority from him.

President Hoover discussed the subject again in a

message to Congress under date of December 19, 1932.[5] His conclusions were summarized as follows:

"Thus from this present complex situation certain definite conclusions are unavoidable:

"1. A number of the most serious problems have now arisen and we are bound to recognize and deal with them.

"2. It is of great importance that preparatory action should be taken at once otherwise time will be lost while destructive forces are continuing against our agriculture, employment and business.

"3. Adequate and proper machinery for dealing with them must be created. It is clear that ordinary diplomatic agencies and facilities are not suitable for the conduct of negotiations which can best be carried on across the table by specially qualified representatives.

"4. As I have pointed out, the discussion of debts is necessarily connected with the solution of major problems at the World Economic Conference and the Arms Conference. The ideal way would therefore seem to be that some of our representatives in these matters should be selected at once who can perform both these functions of preparing for the World Economic Conference, and should exchange views upon the debt questions with certain nations at once and to advise upon the course to be pursued as to others. It would be an advantage for some of them to be associated with the Arms Conference.

[5] *State Papers*, Vol. II, pp. 547–554.

Some part of the delegates appointed for this purpose could well be selected from the members of the Congress. On the side of the Executive this is no derogation of either Executive authority or independence; on the side of the Congress it is no commitment but provides for the subsequent presentation to the Congress of the deliberations, intricacies, reasoning and facts upon which recommendations have been based and is of first importance in enabling the Congress to give adequate consideration to such conclusions.

"5. Discussions in respect to both debt questions and the World Economic Conference cannot be concluded during my Administration, yet the economic situation in the world necessitates the preliminary work essential to its success. The undertaking of these preliminary questions should not be delayed until after March 4.

"I propose, therefore, to seek the co-operation of President-elect Roosevelt in the organization of machinery for advancement of consideration of these problems.

"A year ago I requested that the Congress should authorize the creation of a Debt Commission to deal with situations which were bound to arise. The Congress did not consider this wise. In the situation as it has developed it appears necessary for the Executive to proceed. Obviously any conclusions would be subject to approval by the Congress.

"On the other hand should the Congress prefer to

authorize by legislative enactment a commission set up along the lines above indicated it would meet my hearty approval. . . .

"The situation is one of such urgency that we require national solidarity and national co-operation if we are to serve the welfare of the American people and indeed if we are to conquer the forces which today threaten the very foundations of civilization."

President Hoover at once reopened correspondence with President-elect Roosevelt,[6] and proposed that the latter should join in the selection of a Commission to work out the above problem. But the Democratic leaders, who were in consultation with Roosevelt, refused to join in the creation of such a Commission or to approve its purposes. The position of the President-elect should be stated in his own words and in the following telegram.

"Albany, N. Y.
"December 21, 1932

"THE PRESIDENT
"The White House
"Dear Mr. President:

"I think perhaps the difficulties to which you refer are not in finding the means or the willingness for co-operation but, rather, in defining clearly those things concerning which co-operation between us is possible.

"We are agreed that commitments to any particular policy prior to March fourth are for many reasons in-

[6]This may be found in full in Myers and Newton, pp. 290–297.

advisable and indeed impossible. There remains therefore before that date only the possibility of exploratory work and preliminary surveys.

"Please let me reiterate not only that I am glad to avoid the loss of precious time through delay in starting these preliminaries but also that I shall gladly receive such information and expression of opinion concerning all of those international questions which because of existing economic and other conditions must and will be among the first concerns of my Administration.

"However, for me to accept any joint responsibility in the work of exploration might well be construed by the debtor or other nations, collectively and individually, as a commitment—moral even though not legal, as to policies and courses of action.

"The designation of a man or men of such eminence as your telegram suggests would not imply mere fact-finding; it would suggest the presumption that such representatives were empowered to exchange views on matters of large and binding policy.

"Current press dispatches from abroad already indicate that the joint action which you propose would most certainly be interpreted there as much more of a policy commitment than either you or I actually contemplate.

"May I respectfully suggest that you proceed with the selection of your representatives to conduct the preliminary exploration necessary with individual debtor nations and representatives to discuss the agenda of the World Economic Conference, making it clear that none of these representatives is authorized to bind this Government as to any ultimate policy.

"If this is done, let me repeat that I shall be happy to receive their information and their expressions of opinion.

"To that I add the thought that between now and March fourth I shall be very glad if you will keep me advised as to the progress of the preliminary discussions, and I also shall be happy to consult with you freely during this period.

(Signed) "FRANKLIN D. ROOSEVELT."

"9:45 P.M."

It was unreasonable to expect Hoover to appoint a delegation to formulate or present policies which might be repudiated entirely and within a few months. No foreign government would consider dealing with such a delegation as a serious matter. However, Hoover informed Roosevelt that he would appoint to such a delegation any experienced men whom the latter might suggest. As distorted versions of the correspondence and discussions were appearing daily, Hoover considered it would be less harmful if full publication were made. On December 22 he gave out the complete correspondence to representatives of the press at Washington with the following statement :[7]

[7]*State Papers*, Vol. II, pp. 554–559.

"Governor Roosevelt considers that it is undesirable for him to assent to my suggestions for co-operative action on the foreign problems outlined in my recent message to Congress. I will respect his wishes.

"Situations will no doubt develop and will be dealt with by the Administration as they arise, but of course no commitments will be made for the next Administration.

"The correspondence between myself and Governor Roosevelt is attached hereto."

There can be no question that the failure to act promptly, and upon a united front with the object of currency stabilization and an adjustment of war debts, impeded world recovery. It also was an added obstacle to a return, by the world, to stable monetary standards.

XII

DISCUSSIONS WITH PRESIDENT-ELECT ROOSEVELT

II. RELATIONS WITH GREAT BRITAIN AND FRANCE

THE RESULT of the correspondence and personal conferences between President Hoover and President-elect Roosevelt, as told in the preceding chapter, was to leave the situation in regard to our foreign affairs decidedly up in the air. Hoover, with a deep sense of responsibility, felt that although his own term of office had only two more months to run something should be done to relieve the uncertainties which were threatening the whole conduct of our foreign relations. He was willing to do anything and everything possible to make as easy as possible the transition from one Administration to another. Roosevelt called Hoover on the telephone and suggested an appointment for some time about January 19, 1933.

On January 13, 1933, following a meeting of his Cabinet, Hoover made the following personal note:

"After Cabinet I raised the question with Stimson and Mills of sending a note to the French, again demanding payment of the debt installment. I stated it was necessary that we should not let them think that the American people were giving way and were not serious about our demands, that we had to maintain the integrity of these agreements, that the French had the least justification of anybody for their action, that they had ample money and capacity to pay, that they were engaged in misrepresentation and propaganda which should be brought to an end by a perfectly clear, historical and positive statement of the American position. Stimson demurred but Mills agreed that such a note should be written and undertook that the Treasury would formulate such a note."

The next day, January 14, Secretary of State Stimson reported conversations which he had held with the President-elect, upon the suggestion of the latter, concerning the questions of war debts and international stabilization. Secretary Stimson now made a written report to President Hoover to the following effect. He stated that in his telephone conversation with Roosevelt he had told the President-elect that he (Stimson) had been working hard on the matter which he had been discussing and that he would try to state to him the difficulties and dangers which were found in his plan. He enumerated them at length and then gave to Roosevelt the suggestions which the Administration would make in order to meet them.

Stimson said that the difficulties were as follows:

Even if the debt negotiations were handled separately from the Economic Conference as Roosevelt in his personal conference with the President had previously suggested, nevertheless, Roosevelt would want to be sure, in advance, of British co-operation in the conference before he should be willing to agree to a definite debt settlement. Stimson pointed out, for example, that the United States would wish to secure the assurance of Great Britain that she would stabilize sterling as a means of raising world prices. This would be one of the parts of the Economic Conference. It would be a great advantage to us unless our nation proposed to join in the race for national inflation which was now going on among the nations, and this he assumed that Roosevelt would not wish to do. Roosevelt at once said that of course he did not want to join such a race. Stimson then pointed out that unless we could be sure that Britain would agree to stabilize, we would not want to give up our debts beforehand. Roosevelt said he could see this perfectly and agreed. Stimson also pointed out that for this reason it would be necessary for the British representative who might come over to discuss this matter with us to be prepared on this question and he would have to know this beforehand. Roosevelt agreed to this also. Stimson observed that unless we had a general British and American understanding before a conference, this conference would be likely to fail. Co-operation between the two nations was virtually necessary for the success of the conference as a whole. Roosevelt was very emphatic and cordial upon this and agreed perfectly.

In the second place, Stimson reminded Roosevelt that when he conferred with him a few days previously he had suggested that it was probable that so far as Great Britain was concerned this could not be a one man conference. The British would probably want to send over several men and prepare them beforehand with regard to the line of discussion. Roosevelt said he could see that but hoped we could keep the number of the British down to the smallest possible. He did not want them to send over too many delegates. Stimson said that the Administration would do the best it could but it would be difficult to control the British upon such a matter as that.

Stimson told Roosevelt in the third pace that such a conference would take time and continuous session and that we could not keep the important British representatives who might come here sitting around idle between intermittent discussions with them. We should have to have on our part people ready here to confer continuously. Roosevelt said he could understand that and agreed to do it.

In the fourth place, Stimson told Roosevelt that of course the Hoover representatives could not negotiate. All they could do was the preparatory work of investigation, *et cetera*, in order to lay the foundations for his negotiations. Roosevelt agreed at once. Stimson now said that this conference had been Roosevelt's proposition but he was sure that, very early in the meeting with the British, some type of negotiation was likely to appear. At least very early in the conversations there would be stated the plans which each side might have and the American plan must be Roosevelt's plan and not Hoover's plan. This, of course, Roosevelt agreed to.

Finally, and in the fifth place, Stimson said that if the conference was held in Washington there would be the danger that the press and various members of Congress might begin sniping at the conference just as soon as this stage of the negotiations was reached and a disclosure of the respective plans was made. These plans would surely leak out and would meet with opposition from these sources. Roosevelt said he could see that.

On the other hand, and in contrast to the above, Stimson made the following points with regard to the difficulties which lay in the way and with a view to meeting the views of Roosevelt as far as possible and yet avoid the dangers which were inherent in these conditions. The British probably would not arrive here before March 1. By that time Roosevelt would have chosen his Secretary of State and Secretary of the Treasury and they would be the ones who could meet the British. Before that time, representatives of the Hoover Administration, especially Stimson and Mills, could prepare and consult with Roosevelt and with his incoming Secretaries and get ready the data which would be necessary for use after the British arrived. This would avoid, as far as possible, the idea of a commission, by having the new Secretaries act for Roosevelt. By making an early announcement that a delegation from Great Britain was coming to this country, there would be a psychological advantage which would react upon the country as a help toward recovery. Roosevelt received this suggestion in a friendly manner and seemed to think that this was the best thing that could be done. He made no counter suggestion but told Stimson that he had been having a conference with Russell C. Leffingwell of J. P. Morgan and Company, and that the latter had stated substantially what Stimson also had said.

Stimson urged upon Roosevelt that it would be helpful for him to decide as early as possible the line which his policy would follow, in order that the British might have some knowledge of the type of men they should send over and of the staff which these men should bring with them. Roosevelt said he could understand that. Finally, Stimson stated that he was sure that Hoover would be glad to talk with Roosevelt when he came to Washington. Roosevelt stated that he would arrive in Washington on Thursday, January 19 at about 3:30 P.M. and if the President desired he would come to see him at once on his way from the station or he would drop in to see him the first thing the next morning, whichever Hoover wished. He also asked Stimson if he would call to see him at the Mayflower Hotel. Stimson

225

replied he would come whenever and wherever Roosevelt wished.

President Hoover, after due consideration of the above report, on January 15 sent to Secretary Stimson the following memorandum for his guidance when he conferred again with Mr. Roosevelt.

"I have been thinking over your discussion with Governor Roosevelt and our conferences on the subject. I can express myself best on paper.

"My understanding is that the Governor wishes us to invite some prominent British statesman to come to the United States for purposes of discussing the British debt. He proposes that we carry on the negotiations and he would be glad to see the representative and keep in communication with us.

"This seems to me to disclose the fact that the Governor has not yet comprehended the problem with which the world is confronted and which we have tried to get before him. The question which we have to meet is: Will the United States take a courageous part in the stabilization of the world economic situation? The British debt question is but a small segment of this problem. It should not be discussed except where there is to be a full *quid pro quo* in an effort on the part of Great Britain to bring economic remedy to the world which would alter the course of economic degeneration in the United States. One delegate from the British Government, no matter how eminent, coming to the United States for the purpose of discussion of the debt, could only be disappointed. What is required is a group of the best brains of England, to sit down with a group of the best and most expert brains of the United States to work out a plan to reverse the economic forces now working in the world. This will be a discussion which will take weeks and months. No concession should be given to the British until that project is complete and then only if it shows results to the United States.

"The United States and England should co-operate on this broad question. These two nations jointly could present a program to the World Economic Conference which would meet acceptance and remedy the destructive forces now operating. That can only be done through the collective forces and thought of several Americans and several Englishmen who are going to devote themselves to the pursuit of this question from the day conversations are opened until the completion of the Economic Conference. All this will require preparation and study which will absorb all the time before March 4. The announcement that this is in course is enough to aid the situation temporarily.

"We therefore come back to the fact that if anything effective is to be done, Governor Roosevelt must designate three or more of the men he would like to undertake their own preparations for such negotiations. I would be glad to appoint them if they are men of understanding in these questions. I would be glad to give them every resource of the present Administration, but they must negotiate on behalf of the incoming Administration. Nothing else will carry confidence or effect results. Our original proposal did not contemplate any completed negotiation.

"If an English delegation is to come here they should not arrive before March 1 or until the new Secretaries of the Treasury and State are appointed. Otherwise a negotiation participated in by both administrations will result in the press and every politician trying to drive wedges between the incoming and outgoing administrations during the negotiations. It was for this reason that I proposed that the delegation should prepare and then go to Europe, not negotiate here.

"It seems to me that any other course than the above is a futility and might lead to actual disasters and disappointments which would make the situation even worse.

"If the Governor wants an Englishman to come over and if *he* will do all the negotiating, we can facilitate it."

As already stated, President-elect Roosevelt had expressed a desire further to discuss the matter of the debt with President Hoover and a meeting was arranged for January 20. He stopped off en route to a fishing cruise in Florida waters on Mr. Vincent Astor's yacht. In the meantime, Secretary Stimson had learned that the President-elect had changed his mind as to the British representatives coming at once and had concluded that it was desirable to ask some eminent British statesman to come immediately after the fourth of March.[1]

The conference desired by the President-elect took place on January 20 at the White House. President Hoover immediately afterward dictated a memorandum which was read and confirmed by Secretary of State Stimson and Secretary of the Treasury Mills, who had been present. The memorandum is as follows:

"Conference on January 20, 1933: At the conference at eleven o'clock this morning were Mr. Roosevelt, Secretary Stimson, Secretary Mills, Norman Davis and Mr. Moley. I outlined again briefly the necessity of some indicated course of action or program by the American Government in connection with the international economic situation, first, in order that this vital relief should be put in course of accomplishment, and second, that some hope of stability should be given to

[1] Raymond Moley on Page 94 of his book, *After Seven Years,* makes the following statement. I have abridged it without any change in essential meaning. "The next day, January 17, Governor Roosevelt, without consulting any of us, issued a statement saying that 'American foreign policy must uphold the sanctity of international treaties.' ... It was, in essence, wholehearted acquiescence in the Hoover-Stimson rejection of the traditional American concept of neutrality, of disinterestedness, impartiality, and non-participation in foreign quarrels. Finally, it endorsed a policy that invited a major war in the Far East—a war which the United States and England might have had to wage against Japan had England not refused to go along with Stimson."

It should be said in the most definite way, and without reference to what may have been in the mind of Secretary Stimson, that this statement on the part of Mr. Moley is the exact opposite to the policies and ideas of President Hoover as the record has abundantly shown.

the world by the indication of a definite purpose on the part of the American Government at the earliest moment.

"I reviewed the subject shortly and stated that I understood the Governor wished that the British Government, having asked to take up debt questions, should be informed that the new Administration would be prepared to receive their representatives early in March to discuss the debt question. The Governor agreed that this was his idea and that it should not be confused with the questions before the Economic Conference. I stated that I was convinced that the debt question was but a segment of the whole international economic problem, and that if we were to make any sacrifice in connection with debt it must be made in exchange for positive *quid pro quo* to the American people of positive and definite order; that the debt question could not be separated without sacrifice of American interests; that the invitation to the British to send a representative on debts alone, as he proposed, would lead simply to discussion of reduction of debt, out of which the British had everything to gain and we had everything to lose.

"I reiterated that it was absolutely vital that the American people should receive definite and positive *quid pro quo* (and I repeated this several times) for any adjustments or concessions made in respect to the debt; that it was impracticable to discuss the debt without discussing these compensations; that among these compensations were many of the problems which were before the World Economic Conference; that it was vitally necessary for us to have agreement as to what line the British would take. I stated that there were other forms of compensations which should be required.

"I also suggested that united action between Great Britain and the United States, as the two greatest commercial countries in the world, in a program to be laid before the Economic Conference for the rehabilitation of the situation, would make the conference a success. I pointed out that such leadership would be followed by the entire world, and that it was the only road to stability, the only way to turn the tide in price levels and thus halt the degeneration now going on.

"There were other questions of compensation besides those at the Economic Conference that might well be raised in such a discussion, and I do not see how debt questions could be separated from the compensations.

"Governor Roosevelt again stated that he felt that the debts and the Economic Conference should be kept separated. His view was that a British representative should come to the United States for the purpose of discussion of debts, and that the other questions might arise naturally in the course of such discussion.

"Secretary Stimson pointed out with emphasis that it could not be indicated to the British that we would receive their representative to discuss debts and then later raise these vital questions; that the British would at once take advantage of the situation that they had not been forewarned, that other collateral questions would be raised; that if he intended to raise such questions, the British must be informed of it before starting and that if he did not intend to raise them he would find himself and the United States simply losing on the debts with nothing to come to the American people.

"Secretary Mills pointed out the propaganda being issued from the British Treasury to the effect that they were not prepared to give any compensations, and that they had only one view—cancellation or major reduction. He reiterated that the debts were our only weapon to secure stability and compensations, that no debt settlement ever ought to be made until all these were absolutely secured.

"I pointed out again that no single man could represent all these questions; that the British Government should be notified so that they could bring a number of men adapted to the problems which would come up; and that the United States should be prepared to meet them with effective personnel.

"I felt that it would be very desirable for some man of the stature of Mr. Baldwin or Mr. MacDonald to come, but he would have to be accompanied by others if they were going to compass the problem which really confronted us; that it would be a long and tedious negotiation and I pointed out the history of the Arms Conference, where we had settled the major issues before Mr. MacDonald came to the United States but that it took seven months of hard negotiation.

"Professor Moley kept insisting that the two things must be kept separate. He admitted that perhaps if two separate representatives were sent on the two subjects at the same time they could be discussed separately. He stated that if one representative came on debts and another on economic questions, they could discuss the different questions in different rooms and thus maintain the separation.

"Governor Roosevelt suggested that he personally would discuss the debt questions, and that naturally the departmental officials would discuss the economic question, but that there ought to be a separation in the matter.

"The Secretary of State reaffirmed that no concessions on the debts should be made until he had secured a *quid pro quo* in forms which would compensate the American people, and that thus both subjects should be dealt with together, whether by separate delegations or by one. I pointed out that if they had separate delegations they would co-ordinate themselves even if the Americans did not do so.

"Mr. Mills stated again that he could not then separate the discussions.

"Norman Davis agreed that they could not be separated.

"I realized it was now a question of saving the Governor's face in view of his public statements, and I stated that often enough these were questions of a formula, and that we might try to arrive at a formula for an invitation.

"Professor Moley and Governor Roosevelt objected to the formula proposed as being too obvious a connection of the debt question with other economic questions; that it might involve us in determining the agenda of the Economic Conference. They wished to keep these matters entirely separate. Davis pointed out that the agenda was merely a menu and meant nothing. I stated that the big thing was the *quid pro quo*.

"During the conversation, some cables from Ambassador Sackett at Geneva had been brought to Secretary Stimson. The Secretary read portions of them aloud and pointed out that in these cables we were now warned that the British intended to insist that the British debt must be settled before and as a separate matter from the consideration of any of these other economic questions; that, therefore, unless we gave notice that we held a contrary view and should insist on it, the British were likely to refuse to discuss these economic matters when they were here for the debts. Secretary Stimson showed these cables in their entirety during the conference to Professor Moley and to Mr. Davis, besides reading portions of them aloud at the conference.

"We again went over the ground that these things could not be separated, pointing out this was a drive to get debt reductions without a *quid pro quo* and that it was sacrificing our interests.

"Finally, I suggested that it was the President-elect's wish and that we would of course send anything he wanted, but that we had given him our opinion—that personal negotiation by the President was wrong and would lead to trouble.

"It was settled that somewhat the following would be sent, but that it did not meet our views. I took it down:

" 'The British Government has asked for a discussion of the debts. The incoming Administration will be glad to receive their representative early in March for this purpose. It is, of course, necessary to discuss at the same time the world economic problems in which the United States and Great Britain are mutually interested, and therefore that representatives should also be sent to discuss ways and means for improving the world situation.'

"This seemed to meet the Governor's desires. He pointed out that split into two sentences it showed that the two subjects were separate.

"Secretary Mills again pointed out that the British Government must be informed that the two subjects were indissolvable and they would have to send representatives on both subjects and not upon one alone.

"The Governor suggested that the Secretary of State should inform the British Government of this verbally.

"The Secretary of State then insisted upon having

concrete instructions as to what he was to say to the British Ambassador. The Governor and Mr. Moley agreed that he was to insist verbally to the Ambassador that the two subjects in the two different sentences were indissolvable, that one purpose could not be accepted without the other.

"In order that there should be no misunderstanding, the Secretary of State repeated that it was his instructions that he should inform the British Ambassador that in reply to their request for discussion of the debt, President Roosevelt would receive their representative early in March for such discussion, but at the same time the whole compensations must be discussed and considered at that time; that the British were to be clearly informed that we expect in this discussion that there should be a compensation that is a *quid pro quo* to the American people in any adjustment, and that they should not send representatives to the United States under any misapprehension as to our purpose.

"It was agreed that the Secretary of State and Mr. Moley would draft the invitation to the British.

"Some other questions were discussed not pertinent to this matter."

The following personal memoranda are in the private papers of Hoover. Their inclusion at this point will further indicate the plans that Hoover had in mind and also the tenuous course of the negotiation, both domestic and foreign.

"January 21, 1933 (Saturday).

"I asked Stimson and Mills to come to a meeting at the White House at 6 o'clock and I again raised the question of the note to the French, stating that it was vital from the point of view of the American people that such a note should be sent, that I regretted the delays that had taken place and that the matter must be taken in hand at once.

"Secretary Stimson said that Governor Roosevelt was opposed to sending such a note: I said that he could not take the position that we should not defend the interests of Americans. It was assumed that the French would pay the money immediately on Governor Roosevelt's inauguration as a compliment to him and as a slap at the present Administration. I stated that I was not going to be a party to such things as that. The French were trying to avoid payment and as long as we were in office we had the responsibility to the people in this matter and I proposed to go straight down the road with it. A long discussion ensued. Mr. Mills suggested that a courteous reminder should be sent to the French but that it should be submitted to Governor Roosevelt for his approval and that he should be asked to discuss it on the telephone. If the Governor's statements were correctly quoted that he regarded the French on a parity with the British despite their default, it could be pointed out to him in a covering letter that this was doing harm to the American people and that the way to straighten it out was to send such a note and indicate that it had his approval. The form of the note was settled and the matter was agreed upon."

"Sunday, January 22, 1933.

"The Secretary of State called me on the telephone and said that he proposed to call Governor Roosevelt and ask him if he would agree that the Czechs, Italians and other small nations who had paid the December installment could now send delegations. I told him I saw no objection to that but that I did not see any advantage in it. I asked him if the French note had been sent and he stated that he did not propose to send it. A long discussion took place as to the matter and it finally resulted in my giving him positive directions to submit the note to Governor Roosevelt, that if the Governor disapproved of sending the note it at least relieved this Administration from responsibility; if he approved, we would certainly collect the money. I stated that even if he disapproved of the note, I still felt we would need to go ahead with the matter. I told him if the note was sent to the French they would undoubtedly come back with some argument and give us an opportunity to set out clearly and precisely their outrageous conduct in the whole matter and leave a record that would be indelible for all time on the situation.

"About 6 o'clock Mr. Bundy came to see me with the covering letter and the note stating that the Secretary of State had told him to send it at my request. He again wanted to know if I still was of the opinion that it should be sent and I told him it should be sent at once and that I was irritated at the delay that had taken place, that the fog of propaganda coming out from Roosevelt's supporters was hourly undermining our situation with the French."

After the conference on January 20, Secretary Stimson had adjourned to the State Department to draft the invitation to the British in conjunction with Mr. Moley. A note was drafted and submitted to Mr. Roosevelt as follows:

"In our previous correspondence on this subject the British Government has expressed a desire in the near future for a discussion of the debts owed by that Government to the United States. I am authorized by Mr. Roosevelt, the President-elect, to say that he will be glad to receive at Washington a representative or representatives of the British Government for that purpose early in March, and as soon as possible after the inauguration.

"The British Government will, of course, understand from the statements which have been hitherto made by this Government and its representatives that it will be necessary to discuss at the same time all of the compensations and advantages which the American people may expect to secure from the British Government in return for sacrifices for which they may be asked in any

239

settlement based upon these discussions. For that purpose it is evident that it will be necessary to discuss at the same time the world economic problems and other questions in which our two countries are mutually interested, and the ways and means for improving the present world situation. Therefore, to enable the discussions to proceed with promptness and without interruption, it is suggested that the British representatives should come prepared to discuss these problems and that situation."

Mr. Roosevelt, upon the note being submitted, made various suggestions. As the result of these, the note finally handed to the British Ambassador by the Secretary of State, at the request of President-elect Roosevelt, read as follows:

"In our previous correspondence on this subject the British Government has expressed a desire for a discussion in the near future of the debts owed by that Government to the United States. I am authorized by Mr. Roosevelt, the President-elect, to say that he will be glad to receive at Washington a representative or representatives of the British Government for that purpose early in March, as soon as possible after his inauguration.

"Mr. Roosevelt wishes it to be understood that any discussion of the debts which the British Government may wish to bring up must be concurrent with and conditioned upon a discussion of the world economic problems in which the two governments are mutually interested, and therefore that representatives should also be sent at the same time to discuss the ways and means for improving the world situation. "January 20, 1933."

On January 25 the British Government replied as follows to the Secretary of State.[2]

"We have received with great satisfaction the communication sent by the President-elect of the United States through you in reply to our proposal of November 10 for a discussion on the American debt question. We note that Mr. Roosevelt would like to receive a representative or representatives of His Majesty's Government at Washington as soon as possible after March 4. His Majesty's Government are happy to accept this invitation. The effect of the debt situation upon a wide range of world economic problems is crucial to every government and in the course of the discussion at Washington on the debt we shall be glad to take the opportunity of exchanging views with Mr. Roosevelt on those other matters in which the two governments are so closely interested. It will be recognized that decisions on matters which constitute the subject of the approaching World Economic Conference and which affect other States cannot be reached before discussions take place at that conference between all the States represented there."

[2]Dept. of State, Press Release, Weekly Issue No. 174, Jaunary 28, 1933.

The last sentence of this statement demolished any notion of a *quid pro quo*.

In a subsequent Cabinet discussion of the incident, President Hoover expressed complete bewilderment over the continual resistance of Roosevelt to joining debt discussion with compensations in currency stabilization or in reduction of foreign barriers against our agricultural produce. Hoover feared it could only indicate the intentions of the President-elect to undertake devaluation. He suggested that it further indicated a desire to inaugurate the new Administration by staging visits from leading European statesmen which would, of course, be impossible if delegations had already been appointed to handle these troubled subjects in any effective way.

Hoover further prepared for Secretary Stimson the following memorandum, which was sent to Roosevelt by Stimson on January 27, 1933.

"The long experience which I have had in dealing with debt questions leads me to certain anxieties as to the last development.

"The British Government requested a discussion of the debts, and Governor Roosevelt directed that their representative would be received for this purpose. At the same time they were notified that other questions of interest to the American people would also be raised.

"The note of the British Government following the

speech delivered by the British Chancellor of the Exchequer on January 24, when viewed in its relation to the forthcoming discussion between the governments of the United States and Great Britain in respect to the debt, would appear to be an enunciation of the British position as to the basis of such discussion. A situation highly dangerous to the interests of the American people might thereby be created.

"The views of the British Government on the subject of inter-governmental debts and reparations are well known. The British Government believes that debt payments are contingent on reparation payments and that all of these inter-governmental obligations should be cancelled. They have repeatedly expressed these views and have reasserted them in the notes delivered to this Government during the course of the last two months. On the other hand, the position of the United States Government is equally clear. President Wilson first laid down the policy that this Government would recognize no connection between reparation obligations and the debts due this Government, and that the latter constituted solemn engagements which our Government expected would be met. Subsequently, in effecting settlements with each of the individual debtors, our Government established the principle of settling these debts on the basis of the capacity of the debtor to pay—a policy which met with the full approval of the Congress. The position of our Government from the time the debt

the British Government, has stated that while still believing in total cancellation, they are ready to discuss
with us the lines on which a new agreement can be
reached, bearing in mind two things: 'First, that the
settlement to be reached must be the final settlement,
and secondly, that it must be one which will not involve
resumption of the claims on Germany for reparations,
which it was the object of the Lausanne settlement last
year to end.' This can only mean that the kind of discussion which the British Government envisages is the
payment of a comparatively small sum, probably in the
form of a lump sum payment based upon reparations
settlements.

"While it does not say so in so many words, the British note of January 25, if it does not exclude, certainly
does not contemplate basing a new settlement on definite
compensations in the economic field, and there is every
reason to believe the British Treasury will vigorously
oppose any such proposal.

"The views of the two governments thus appear to us
to be so far apart that at least it would seem doubtful
whether they can be reconciled and brought into harmony at a formal conference unless preliminary and
preparatory discussions are to take place. As a matter
of fact, if past experience means anything such preliminary spade work is essential to the successful conclusion of a conference of this character. It is all the
more essential in this case, since failure to reach an

agreement with the British Government would probably mean the collapse of the debt obligations to the United States and their wiping out through default.

"Furthermore, in view of Mr. Chamberlain's very definite speech and the equivocal character of the British note, the question arises whether silence on our part might not lead the British Government to believe that the policies heretofore enunciated by our Government would not be maintained, and we would be accepting their position as the basis of discussion.

"It is my opinion, therefore, that this situation should be clarified, and that failure to do so might imperil the success of the future negotiations and the protection of the interests of our Government. I do not believe that the right way to clarify the situation is through the exchange of formal notes, but rather through informal discussions intended to define the area in which the negotiations are to take place, and to lay the foundation for the agreement which can only be definitely reached by the high officials of the two governments. It would be extremely difficult for such preliminary discussions to be conducted through the existing Administration. They could, however, be undertaken almost at once by Governor Roosevelt's Secretary of State and the Secretary of the Treasury. In our view, if Governor Roosevelt is not in a position to definitely select these officers until, let us say, the middle of February, that it would be wiser to postpone the formal negotiations until a later date in March in order to permit these gentlemen to do the preliminary work which appears to be essential to the ultimate success of the negotiations.

"It is all-important in the interest of the United States that the British Government should understand that we will not under any circumstances accept the British policy of cancellation, or the equivalent of cancellation, or any reparations connection; that we regard these obligations freely entered into by both parties after mature consideration as a binding contract which cannot be set aside by unilateral action, or to be abrogated by a threat of default; that our people regard them as binding, not only from a legal, but from a moral standpoint; and that while we may be willing to discuss them at their request in the light of all the circumstances, we cannot recognize the right of any debtor to compel the making of a new agreement under threat of repudiating an existing solemn agreement, or for them to enumerate the bases of discussion. For us to take any other position would not only place our Government in a hopelessly disadvantageous position in conducting the coming negotiations, but would deal a deadly blow to the sanctity of all international engagements.

"I understand that the British Ambassador is leaving in a day or two for London, and it would seem to me important that he should inform his Government that our Government expects the British representatives to conduct discussion upon our basis as outlined above and suggest that upon his return to the United States he should bring competent assistants to enter upon preliminary discussions with the new Secretaries of State and Treasury, who would probably be known by that time."

From this time forward Roosevelt set up his own relations with the British Ambassador at Washington and carried on his own negotiations directly with the British Government. By the middle of February, Hoover had determined to lay before the country his views upon the subject of international currency relations, as well as upon the necessity of maintaining the gold standard. He did so in a Lincoln Day address delivered in New York City on the thirteenth of that month. It was a report upon the danger which, as he knew, then was facing the American people.[3] It was an utterance of real prophetic character. All the debtors, except heroic little Finland, defaulted. This default led to resistance to any adequate compensation—any adjustment the United States might make in the war debts. Today, they are a "dead horse," with little prospect even of using the carcass for the purposes of fertilizing international trade.

[3]See *State Papers*, Vol. II, pp. 586–595.

XIII

CONCLUSION

THE COMPLETE lack of co-operation, at a time of great national emergency, which was the studied policy of President-elect Roosevelt and the Democratic majority in Congress led by Speaker John N. Garner, continued during the final two months of the Hoover Administration. In the opinion of the most reliable economists, it is a generally accepted judgment that this led directly to the banking crisis and the untold loss and suffering that came to the American people.[1] This is another story that already has been told elsewhere.[2]

[1]Raymond Moley states (in his *Saturday Evening Post* article of July 29, 1939, page 52, entitled "Bank Crisis, Bullet Crisis—and Same Smile") that Hoover offered to co-operate with Roosevelt "in any line of sensible action." This was contained in a letter from Hoover to Roosevelt under date of February 17, 1933. Moley infers in this article and in his book (*After Seven Years*, pp. 140–142), that this offer was unreasonable on the part of Hoover. It would seem that all Hoover was asking of Roosevelt was that the latter should stand by the plain terms of the Democratic National Platform of 1932, upon which he was elected, and should carry out the promises contained in his campaign speeches.

[2]See Myers and Newton, Chapters 18 and 19. Raymond Moley in his book, *After Seven Years* (page 146, note), casts doubt upon the statements in Myers and Newton (page 366), describing a telephone conversation between Hoover and Roosevelt late on the night of March 3, 1933, which exhibited in crass form the unco-operative attitude of Roosevelt. It may be stated that the same conversation, as described by Senator Carter Glass, who was present with Roosevelt at the time, agrees in every essential particular with the statements of Myers and Newton (see *Carter Glass—a Biography*, by Rixey Smith and Norman Beasley, pp. 340–342).

Some time during the month of February, 1933, Secretary of State Stimson prepared a review of the foreign policies of the Hoover Administration which he sent to Hoover. The latter replied on February 14 enclosing a few notes on the article in the form of corrections or additions to the statements therein made, saying to Stimson: "They may be helpful." As these notes contain a clear and authoritative statement by Hoover of the ideas and policies of his Administration, as he himself saw them, they are herewith given in full.

"There are some bases of my own conception of our foreign policy during the past four years and some slants which I feel are perhaps in need of more emphasis.

"Relations with Latin America

"I made a journey through South America prior to inauguration for the purpose of dissipating the fears and antagonisms which had grown up amongst these States as to the intentions and policies of our Government. On our relations, I stated on one occasion:

" 'And in this connection of the relations of great and little nations, may I mention one sinister notion, fear of which I detect in some sections of the press as to policies of the United States bearing basically upon our relationships with our Latin-American neighbors. That is the fear of an era of the mistakenly called dollar diplomacy. The implications that have been colored by

251

that expression are not a part of my conception of international relations. I can say at once that it never has been and ought not to be the policy of the United States to intervene by force to secure or maintain contracts between our citizens and foreign states or their citizens. Confidence in that attitude is the only basis upon which the economic co-operation of our citizens can be welcomed abroad. It is the only basis that prevents cupidity encroaching upon the weakness of nations—but, far more than this, it is the true expression of the moral rectitude of the United States.'

"We further built on this conception by withdrawal of American marines at every point as rapidly as possible from San Domingo, Nicaragua and Haiti. A great number of times during the Administration I have spoken on these themes such as the attached statement and I believe we have, by our diplomatic conduct, completely re-established confidence that we have no notions of aggression or exploitation.

"THE KELLOGG PACT

"I have stated many times that our purpose was to clothe the Kellogg Pact with positive action in the form of moral sanctions. That what we were endeavoring to do was to build up organized and expressed public opinion of the world against violations of the pact as a corollary of the pact. That this required concerted action amongst nations in which we have in the two major

cases taken the lead and secured its firm establishment.
The first case where we secured fairly widespread protest by other nations and in the second case where we
enunciated the doctrine of non-recognition as a tangible
basis of expressed world opinion not only for the moment but as a continuing protest.

"LEAGUE OF NATIONS

"I feel the memorandum gives the impression of too
strong an alliance with the League. I have insisted upon
the aloofness of the United States from the League of
Nations in that the sanctions of the League are those
of force either economic or military, whereas the United
States could not and would not enter into force measures to settle controversies among other countries under
any circumstances. While such action may be necessary
in Europe we felt it was not our part to engage in any
such cases but in cases where our own treaties were involved we could co-operate in moral sanctions. I have
also sought to build up the firm understanding that the
United States would not under any circumstances enter
into an undertaking which would bind it to indetermine
[*sic*] action even of moral sanctions for the unknown
events of the future. In other words we were prepared
to co-operate with moral sanctions in each single instance as it might arise where there was a direct interest
of the United States involved or where there was even a

major danger to world peace by violation of the Kellogg Pact."

Finally and in conclusion, it should be emphasized that during the years 1929 to 1933, Hoover insisted upon adequate, but not excessive military defense. During his Administration 80,000 tons of new naval vessels were completed, and 100,000 tons more were put under construction. The army equipment was mechanized. The air equipment was increased from 2000 to 2800 planes. The total cost of the whole military establishment was held to about $660,000,000 per year, as contrasted with about $1,400,000,000 just prior to the outbreak of the present European War.

In his drive for peace Hoover was constant and energetic. His practical accomplishments were: (a) reversal of the Wilson policies of intervention in Latin-American States; (b) withdrawal of all occupations by our marines and the consequent building of good will in the Western Hemisphere; (c) treaties further limiting the three leading navies of the world, an extension of the Hughes capital ship limitations, to include cruisers, destroyers , and submarines. He urged economic cooperation with other governments.

Hoover rightly opposed all entanglements in Europe and Asia and refused to engage in economic sanctions against other governments. When he left office three great negotiations were under way making for peace. These were concerned with the world land disarmament conference, the world economic conference, and the extension of naval limitations. All were abandoned or failed under Roosevelt.

Never in our history was peace more assured to the American people or did the United States stand higher in the esteem of the world than on March 4, 1933. Hoover's record stands as an open book to be read by the American people.

INDEX

INDEX

visit, 178–189; Moratorium, 186–187, 204; war debts, 187–189, 205–219, 221; 229–249; foreign loans, 189–201; Economic Conference, 202–204, 214–219, 222–236; conferences with F. D. Roosevelt, 205–249

House, Edward M., 8–9, 206
Howe, Louis McHenry, 206
Hughes, Charles E., 15, 254
Hurley, Patrick J., 163–165, 170
Hyde, Arthur M., 163

Japan and Manchuria, 154–169
Jessup, Philip C., 33

Kellogg, Frank B., 15, 20–22, 30, 33, 44–45
Kellogg-Briand Pact, 21–23, 38, 57, 62–63, 84, 85, 87, 141, 148, 153–154, 156, 159, 163, 165, 252–253

Lamont, R. P., 192–197
Latin-America, 251–253
Laval, Premier, 178–189, 202
League of Nations, 18–20, 29–30, 76, 141, 160, 174, 253–254
Leffingwell, R. C., 225
Libby, Frederick J., 37–38
London Conference (1930), *see* Naval limitation

MacDonald, J. Ramsay, 57–70, 73–75, 97–98, 107–108, 138, 151–152, 153, 202–203
MacDonald, Malcolm, 60
McCormick, Ruth Hanna, 37
Mellon, Andrew W., 203
Military stations, 64–65
Mills, Ogden, 177, 180, 184, 210, 212, 221, 224, 229–239

Moley, Raymond, 209–211, 229–239, 250 (note)
Moratorium, 181, 186–187, 204
Morrow, Dwight W., 79
Moses, George H., 99
Munro, Dana G., 49

Naval limitation, 54–65, 71–108, 181, 254
Navy League, 75–79
Nicaragua, 47, 252

Philippine independence, 169–172
Pratt, William D., 79

Reed, David A., 79, 103–104, 183
Relief, European, 10–12
Reparations, 181–183
Robinson, Joseph T., 79, 103, 117
Roosevelt, Franklin D., 40, 49, 53, 127, 152, 197, 199–201, 205–249, 250
Root, Elihu, 27–33, 53
Rowe, L. S., 52–53, 117
Russia, *see* Bolshevism

Sackett, Frederick M., 204
Shearer, William B., 75–79
Stimson, Henry L., 23 (note), 30, 35–36, 45, 74, 79, 150, 152–155, 160–163, 168–169, 176, 183–184, 187, 202, 220–226, 229–242, 244, 251, 254
Supreme Economic Council, 10–12
Swanson, Claude A., 29

Tacna-Arica dispute, 44–45
Tardieu, Premier, 138
Tariff, Smoot-Hawley, 123–128
Tumulty, Joseph P., 2

Walsh, Thomas J., 29, 34

258

INDEX

557